We combated for victory in the empire of reason,

for strong-holds in the imagination.

✿

From *The Convention of Cintra* (1809), William Wordsworth

Published by the Wordsworth Trust

Dove Cottage, Grasmere, Cumbria LA22 9SH

ISBN 978–1–905256–47–1

Designed by Manny Ling

Printed by WM Print, Walsall, West Midlands

Supported by Lancaster University, Arts Council England and the Westmorland Arts Trust

WORDSWORTH, WAR & WATERLOO

WORDSWORTH, WAR & WATERLOO

Edited by Simon Bainbridge and Jeff Cowton

WORDSWORTH TRUST

CONTENTS

PREFACE

Wordsworth, War & Waterloo is a splendid example of the power of partnership. The exhibition builds upon an established relationship between the Wordsworth Trust and Lancaster University, which has enriched the work of both institutions since it was formalised in 2012.

I am grateful for this opportunity to thank a number of people who have made this exhibition possible. Professor Simon Bainbridge of the Department of English and Creative Writing has co-curated the exhibition with the Wordsworth Trust's Curator, Jeff Cowton, allying his expertise in Napoleonic studies with Jeff's unrivalled knowledge of the Wordsworth Trust's manuscript and fine art collection. I would also like to thank my many colleagues in Grasmere whose unseen but essential work goes into making a project such as this a great success.

I am also grateful to Simon, and to Professor Paul F Betz, Pamela Woof, Dr David Blayney Brown, Professor Richard Matlak, Professor Philip Shaw, Jenny Uglow and Donald Coverdale for contributing wonderfully erudite and entertaining essays to accompany the exhibition. We are indebted to them for their gift of knowledge and time.

This publication emerges out of the exhibition of the same name held at the Wordsworth Museum between March and November 2015. The exhibition would not have been possible without the generosity of a number of important lenders. I'm very grateful to all those organisations and individuals listed in the Acknowledgements for their exemplary support.

In addition to their scholarly contribution to *Wordsworth, War & Waterloo*, Lancaster University has provided generous financial support, as has Arts Council England through its Major Partner Museum Programme, and the Westmorland Arts Trust / Cumbria Community Foundation. This has enabled us to realise the full scope of this exhibition, and make it a fitting contribution to the Waterloo 200 celebrations.

Michael McGregor
The Robert Woof Director, The Wordsworth Trust

LIST OF ILLUSTRATIONS

Figure 1. Benjamin Robert Haydon (1786–1846), *Napoleon Musing at St. Helena*, 1830. © National Portrait Gallery, London.

Figure 2. Benjamin Robert Haydon (1786–1846), *Wellington Musing on the Field of Waterloo*, 1839. © National Portrait Gallery, London.

Figure 3. Thomas Lupton (1791–1873) after Benjamin Robert Haydon, *The Hero and his Horse on the Field of Waterloo*, 1843.

Figure 4. Benjamin Robert Haydon (1786–1846), *Wordsworth on Helvellyn*, 1842. © National Portrait Gallery, London.

Figure 5. Isaac Cruikshank (1756–1811), *The Martyr of Equality*, 1793.

Figure 6. James Gillray (1756–1815), *The Grand Coronation Procession of Napoleone the 1st, Emperor of France, from the Church of Notre Dame, Decr 2d 1804*, 1805. © Trustees of the British Museum.

Figure 7. William Wordsworth (1770–1850), *The Prelude*, Book X, 1805, lines 919–42.

Figure 8. James Gillray (1756–1815), *Spanish-Patriots attacking the French-Banditti. — Loyal Britons Lending a lift*, 1808. © Trustees of the British Museum.

Figure 9. Amos Green (1735–1807), *Dove Cottage*, date unknown.

Figure 10. Dorothy Wordsworth (1771–1855), Grasmere journal, 28 November 1801.

Figure 11. William Wordsworth (1770–1850), Alfoxden Notebook, lines towards 'The Ruined Cottage', 1798.

Figure 12. James Gillray (1756–1815), *John Bulls Progress*, 1793. © Trustees of the British Museum.

Figure 13. James Gillray (1756–1815), *The Storm rising; — or — the Republican Flotilla in danger*, 1798. © Trustees of the British Museum.

Figure 14. *A View of the Volunteer Army of Great Britain in 1806–1807*, reproduced with kind permission of Cumbria Archive Centre, Kendal.

Figure 15. *A View of the Volunteer Army of Great Britain in 1806–1807* (detail), reproduced with kind permission of Cumbria Archive Centre, Kendal.

Figure 16. George Cruikshank (1792–1878), *Symptoms of Drilling*, date unknown.

Figure 17. Unknown artist and engraver, *Britannia bringing her Dead Hero to Britannia's shore*, 1806.

Figure 18. Drawing of The Cherry Tree Inn, Wythburn, possibly by Dora Wordsworth (1804–1847). © Professor Paul F Betz.

Figure 19. Unknown artist, portrait of Annette Vallon.

Figure 20. Drawing of Napoleon in a letter from Heugh Parry to William Wordsworth, 29 July 1815.

Figure 21. Map of the Battlefield of Waterloo. Belonging to David and Janet Bromley.

Figure 22. Joseph Mallord William Turner (1775–1851), from *Waterloo and Rhine Sketchbook*, 1817. © Tate, London 2015.

Figure 23. Joseph Mallord William Turner (1775–1851), *The Field of Waterloo*, 1818. © Tate, London 2015.

Figure 24. James Gillray (1756–1815), *The Zenith of French Glory; — The Pinnacle of Liberty*, 1793. © Trustees of the British Museum.

Figure 25. James Gillray (1756–1815), *Maniac Raving's — or — Little Boney in a strong Fit*, 1803. © Trustees of the British Museum.

Figure 26. James Gillray (1756–1815), *The Corsican-Pest; — or — Belzebub going to Supper*, 1803. © Trustees of the British Museum.

Figure 27. James Gillray (1756–1815), *Buonaparte, 48 hours after Landing*, 1803. © Trustees of the British Museum.

Figure 28. James Gillray (1756–1815), *The Plumb-pudding in danger; — or — State Epicures taking un Petit Souper*, 1805. © Trustees of the British Museum.

ACKNOWLEDGEMENTS

WE WOULD LIKE to thank the following people and organisations for their generosity in lending artefacts to the exhibition *Wordsworth, War & Waterloo:* Carlisle Library; Cumbria's Museum of Military Life; David and Diana Matthews; David Alexander; David and Janet Bromley; Donald Coverdale; Professor Keith Hanley; the Lancashire Infantry Museum; the Liverpool Victoria Gallery and Museum; the National Portrait Gallery; Nick and Dr Cecilia Powell; Paul Heap; Tate Britain and Trinity College, Cambridge.

We would like to thank the following people for sharing their knowledge and ideas, and for giving their time: Amy Concannon; Ann Dinsdale; Christopher Bacon; COL Scott Krawczyk; Constance Parrish; Dr David Spadafora; David Unsworth; Hannah Phillip and Fairfax House; Hazel Clarke; Jane Davies; Jules Wooding; Kate Taylor; Dr Lucy Peltz; Marion Watts; Matthew Clough; Dr Ruth Abbott; Professor Sally Bushell; Stephen White; Stuart Eastwood; Sue Allan and Trent Leinenbach. We would also like to thank Armour Systems™, part of Conservation by Design Ltd, for helping us with the exhibition displays.

Special thanks go to Melissa Mitchell, Assistant to the Curator, for her meticulous preparation of the text and sourcing of images for this book, and to Dr Manny Ling for his beautiful design.

Finally, we would also like to thank our funders for their generosity: Lancaster University and Arts Council England, whose financial support turned an idea into a reality; and the Westmorland Arts Trust / Cumbria Community Foundation, who enabled us to improve our display facilities for the great benefit of this and future exhibitions.

Textual Note: Unless otherwise stated, all quotations from William Wordsworth's poetry are taken from volumes in the Cornell Wordsworth edition, general editor Stephen Maxwell Parrish (Ithaca, New York: Cornell University Press, 1975–2007).

CONTRIBUTORS

SIMON BAINBRIDGE IS Professor of Romantic Studies in the Department of English and Creative Writing, Lancaster University, where he is also Co-Director of the Wordsworth Centre. He is the author of the monographs *Napoleon and English Romanticism* (Cambridge University Press, 1995) and *British Poetry and the Revolutionary and Napoleonic Wars: Visions of Conflict* (Oxford University Press, 2003) as well as numerous essays on the relationship between Romantic literature and the Napoleonic Wars.

Paul F Betz is Professor of English at Georgetown University, Washington DC, USA. He is a Wordsworth scholar who, beginning in 1966, has repeatedly used the resources of the Wordsworth Library in Grasmere. He is the editor of the Cornell Wordsworth series volume *Benjamin the Waggoner* (1981 and 1988). He has long been an enthusiastic collector of Romantic Period books and manuscripts.

Dr David Blayney Brown is Manton Curator of British Art 1790–1850 at Tate Britain. He is leader and senior editor of Tate's online catalogue *J.M.W. Turner: Sketchbooks, Drawings and Watercolours* and has curated many exhibitions including *Turner and Byron* (Tate, 1992), *Benjamin Robert Haydon* (with Robert Woof and Stephen Hebron, the Wordsworth Trust, 1996), *Constable to Delacroix* (with Patrick Noon and Christine Riding, Tate, 2003) and *Late Turner: Painting Set Free* (with Sam Smiles and Amy Concannon, Tate, 2014). His books include *Romanticism* (Phaidon, 2001).

Donald Coverdale is a retired coroner from North Yorkshire. He began collecting eighteenth-and nineteenth-century caricatures while he was a law student in London in the 1970s and now has a significant collection of the works of James Gillray. He is delighted to loan some of these to the Wordsworth Trust.

Richard Matlak is Professor of English at the College of the Holy Cross in Worcester, Massachusetts, USA. He is the author or editor of five books and many essays, mainly on the Wordsworths and Coleridge. His edition of Wordsworth's *Poems, in Two Volumes* (1807) is forthcoming (Broadview Press, 2015).

Philip Shaw is Professor of Romantic Studies at the University of Leicester. He is the author of *Waterloo and the Romantic Imagination* (Palgrave, 2002), *Suffering and Sentiment in Romantic Military Art* (Ashgate, 2013) and the editor of *Romantic Wars: Studies in Culture and Conflict* (Ashgate, 2000).

Jenny Uglow grew up in Cumbria. She is a writer, publisher and Trustee of the Wordsworth Trust. Her books include biographies of Elizabeth Gaskell and Thomas Bewick, *The Lunar Men* (Faber & Faber, 2002), and she has recently published a 'crowd biography', *In These Times: Living in Britain through Napoleon's Wars, 1793–1815* (Faber & Faber, 2014).

Pamela Woof is a former lecturer in English Literature in the Department of Lifelong Learning, Newcastle University, and is President of the Wordsworth Trust. She recently curated the exhibition, *Dorothy Wordsworth, Wonders of the Everyday*, for the Wordsworth Trust, and her edition of the *Grasmere and Alfoxden Journals* (Oxford University Press, 1991) is now the standard classic edition.

CHRONOLOGY

1769	Births of Arthur Wellesley (later Duke of Wellington) and Napoleon Bonaparte.
1770	Birth of William Wordsworth.
1775–83	American War of Independence.
1789	Fall of the Bastille, start of French Revolution.
1790	Wordsworth undertakes walking tour of France and Switzerland.
1791–2	Wordsworth again in France. Witnesses Revolutionary celebrations. Relationship with Annette Vallon and birth of Caroline, their daughter. Wordsworth returns to England.
1793	Louis XVI executed. Outbreak of war between Britain and France. Wordsworth writes republican pamphlet *A Letter to the Bishop of Llandaff* and 'Salisbury Plain'. Start of 'Reign of Terror' in France (until 1794).
1797	Wordsworth writes 'The Ruined Cottage'. Napoleon defeats Austrian army in Italy. French threaten invasion of Britain (until 1798).
1798	Anonymous publication of *Lyrical Ballads*, jointly authored by Wordsworth and Coleridge. Wordsworth begins *The Prelude* while in Germany. France invades Switzerland. British navy (under Nelson) defeats French at Battle of the Nile.
1799	Wordsworth and his sister Dorothy settle at Dove Cottage, Grasmere. Napoleon Bonaparte seizes power in France as First Consul.
1802	Peace of Amiens between Britain and France (until 1803). Wordsworth and Dorothy travel to France to meet Annette and Caroline. Napoleon becomes Consul for Life. Wordsworth marries Mary Hutchinson.
1803	French threaten invasion of Britain. Wordsworth joins Grasmere Volunteers.
1804	Napoleon becomes Emperor of France.
1805	Battle of Trafalgar and death of Admiral Lord Nelson. End of invasion threat. Major French victories at battles of Ulm and Austerlitz.
1806	Wordsworth writes *Benjamin the Waggoner* (published 1819).
1807	Wordsworth publishes *Poems, in Two Volumes*, including 'Sonnets Dedicated to Liberty'. French invasion of Portugal signals start of Peninsular War.
1808	Britain commits troops to Iberian Peninsula to combat French force and support Spanish risings. Wordsworth begins pamphlet on *Convention of Cintra* (published 1809).
1812	Napoleon invades Russia but retreats with huge losses.
1813	Wellington victorious in Peninsular War. Napoleon defeated at Battle of Leipzig.
1814	Napoleon abdicates; exiled to Elba. Wordsworth publishes *The Excursion*.
1815	Napoleon escapes from Elba. After the 'Hundred Days', he is defeated at Battle of Waterloo by combined British and Prussian forces led by Wellington and Blücher. Napoleon exiled to St. Helena. Wordsworth, Southey and their families celebrate on Skiddaw. Wordsworth publishes *Poems*, including second part of 'Sonnets Dedicated to Liberty'.
1816	Wordsworth publishes 'Ode. The Morning of the Day Appointed for a General Thanksgiving. January 18, 1816'.
1820	Wordsworth visits battlefield of Waterloo.
1821	Death of Napoleon.
1850	Death of Wordsworth. Publication of *The Prelude*.
1852	Death of Wellington.

William Wordsworth, 'To B. R. Haydon, Esq. on Seeing His Picture of Napoleon Buonaparte on the Island of St. Helena', 1831

HAYDON! let worthier judges praise the skill

Here by thy pencil shown in truth of lines

And charm of colours; *I* applaud those signs

Of thought, that give the true poetic thrill;

That unencumbered whole of blank and still,

Sky without cloud — ocean without a wave;

And the one Man that laboured to enslave

The World, sole-standing high on the bare hill —

Back turned, arms folded, the unapparent face

Tinged, we may fancy, in this dreary place

With light reflected from the invisible sun

Set like his fortunes; but not set for aye

Like them. The unguilty Power pursues his way,

And before *him* doth dawn perpetual run.

Figure 1. Benjamin Robert Haydon (1786–1846), *Napoleon Musing at St. Helena*, 1830.
© National Portrait Gallery, London.

Figure 2. Benjamin Robert Haydon (1786–1846), *Wellington Musing on the Field of Waterloo*, 1839.
© National Portrait Gallery, London.

William Wordsworth, 'On a Portrait of the Duke of Wellington, upon the Field of Waterloo, by Haydon', 1840

By Art's bold privilege Warrior and War-horse stand
On ground yet strewn with their last battle's wreck;
Let the Steed glory while his Master's hand
Lies fixed for ages on his conscious neck;
But by the Chieftain's look, though at his side
Hangs that day's treasured sword, how firm a check
Is given to triumph and all human pride!
Yon trophied Mound shrinks to a shadowy speck
In his calm presence! Him the mighty deed
Elates not, brought far nearer the grave's rest,
As shows that time-worn face, for he such seed
Has sown as yields, we trust, the fruit of fame
In Heaven; hence no one blushes for thy name,
Conqueror, 'mid some sad thoughts, divinely blest!

Figure 3. Thomas Lupton (1791–1873) after Benjamin Robert Haydon, *The Hero and his Horse on the Field of Waterloo*, 1843.

Haydon's portrait of Wordsworth was painted in response to the poet's sonnet 'On a Portrait of the Duke of Wellington, upon the Field of Waterloo, by Haydon' (see opposite). Wordsworth had composed this sonnet in 1840 whilst ascending Helvellyn with his daughter Dora and her husband Edward Quillinan. The poet was seventy years of age. Quillinan writes in a letter that: 'I wish you could have seen the Old Poet, seated from time to time, as we paused for breath, on a rock writing down his Waterloo Sonnet'.

Figure 4. Benjamin Robert Haydon (1786–1846), *Wordsworth on Helvellyn*, 1842.
© National Portrait Gallery, London.

WORDSWORTH, WAR & WATERLOO

SIMON BAINBRIDGE

WILLIAM WORDSWORTH AND his family celebrated the Battle of Waterloo by joining the public rejoicing that was held on 21 August 1815 on the summit of Skiddaw, the mountain above Keswick in the northern Lake District. Wordsworth's friend and fellow poet Robert Southey, who was also present, wrote an account of the celebration, commenting that 'It is the first time that any public rejoicings had ever been held on so elevated a spot; & the effect was sublime to a degree which none can imagine but those who witnessed it.' A large crowd assembled for the merriment, dancing round a bonfire and watching as large balls of 'tow [flax] and turpentine' were set on fire and rolled down the steep sides of the mountain. The company ate 'beef roasted and plum pudding boiled', sang 'God Save the King' and 'Rule Britannia', and toasted the Prince Regent, the Duke of Wellington and Prince Blücher, with each toast being marked by the firing of a cannon. The festivities concluded at midnight in Keswick with a fireworks display and the launching of a fire balloon inscribed with the names Wellington and Waterloo.[1]

This was a time of national jubilation. The combined British and Prussian victory over Napoleon's French army on 18th June 1815 in farmlands south of Brussels had brought to an end twenty-two years of almost uninterrupted war, fought on a global and unprecedented scale. Britain's conflict with Revolutionary France, which had begun in February 1793, had transformed into an epic struggle against the imperial forces of Napoleon, who had seized power in a *coup d'état* in 1799 and crowned himself Emperor in 1804. The conflict had dominated British life for more than two decades. At the height of the war effort, as many as one in five of all British adult males was involved in the armed forces in either a voluntary or an enrolled position (William Wordsworth had been one such volunteer), while one in four families had members directly involved in the conflict.[2] Though Britain was itself removed from the scenes of fighting, it was subject to major invasion scares in 1797–8 and 1803–5, and there were innumerable daily indications of the national struggle, including the building of barracks and Martello towers, the drilling and encampment of militia and volunteer forces, illuminations to celebrate victories, naval manoeuvres, and the presence of soldiers and sailors returned from the war. The conflict had a profound impact on the British people, as described by Jenny Uglow in her essay in this volume, and its effects were powerfully felt in the village of Grasmere, seemingly remote as it was from the theatre of war, as Pamela Woof illustrates in her essay on Dorothy Wordsworth.

The MARTYR of EQUALITY

Behold the Progress of our System

Figure 5. Isaac Cruikshank (1756–1811), *The Martyr of Equality*, 1793.

For William Wordsworth, the 'victory sublime' of Waterloo was a matter of poetic as well as political and personal significance. As he wrote in his 'Thanksgiving Ode',[3] at Waterloo:

> Imagination, ne'er before content,
> But aye ascending, restless in her pride,
> From all that man's performance could present,
> Stoops to that closing deed magnificent,
> And with the embrace is satisfied. [163–7]

Here Wordsworth presents Waterloo not only as affording a worthy historical culmination to the years of conflict — it is a 'closing deed magnificent' — but also as providing unprecedented 'satisfaction' for the principal poetic power of the 'Imagination'. For Wordsworth, the imagination was the creative, transforming and visionary power that he saw as central not only to poetry but to life more generally, a force that linked the individual to the eternal, universal and divine. In these lines in his 'Ode', Wordsworth claims that while the imagination may seek to transcend human history, it is only with the final defeat of Napoleon that it becomes 'content'. For Wordsworth the imagination had come to play a vital part in both his own and the nation's struggle against France.

Wordsworth's celebration of Waterloo and of the imagination's role in the victory over France would have seemed unthinkable at the conflict's opening (a period in the poet's life discussed by Philip Shaw in his essay in this volume). In 1793, when war broke out between Britain and France, Wordsworth was a passionate supporter of the French Revolution, having experienced revolutionary festivities first hand during his visit to France in 1791–2, famously later describing how 'Bliss was it in that dawn to be alive / But to be young was very heaven' [*Prelude* X, 692–3].[4] In the early months of 1793, the young poet had written (though would never publish) his political pamphlet *A Letter to the Bishop of Llandaff*, in which he described himself as 'the advocate of republicanism' [*Prose Works* I, 38] and defended the execution of Louis XVI, who had been guillotined in January. (See fig. 5 for a contemporary illustration of this event.) For Wordsworth, Britain was aligning itself with the Prussian and Austrian monarchical dynasties which sought to crush the nascent revolutionary nation. He even went so far as to revel in early British defeats, as he later shame-facedly recalled in his poetic autobiography *The Prelude*:

> I rejoiced,
> Yea, afterwards, truth painful to record!
> Exulted in the triumph of my soul
> When Englishmen by thousands were o'erthrown,
> Left without glory on the Field, or driven,
> Brave hearts, to shameful flight. [X, 258–63]

While the next twenty-two years of war saw a major transformation in Wordsworth's political allegiances and in his response to the Anglo-Gallic conflict, they also saw his remarkable development as a poet. Indeed, the major period of Wordsworth's poetic career can be defined through the key dates of the war, beginning in 1793 with the publication of his first volumes (*An Evening Walk* and *Descriptive Sketches*) and running until 1815, the year of Waterloo, when he produced the first collected edition of his works, *Poems, by William Wordsworth*. For Wordsworth, the war with France became at times an overwhelming preoccupation, providing the subject for much of his writing and definitively shaping his poetic identity and career.

Even prior to the outbreak of the Anglo-Gallic conflict, Wordsworth was drawn to the casualties of war as a poetic subject. In *An Evening Walk*, written in 1788–9, he introduced one of the many non-combatant victims of war that would become a characteristic feature of his great poems of the 1790s, in this case a widow whose husband lay 'on Bunker's charnel hill afar' (a reference to a battle in the American War of Independence), leaving her to drag 'her babes along this weary way' [*An Evening Walk* 244–54]. While such suffering figures might be seen as a fairly conventional feature of the poetry of sensibility popular in the second half of the eighteenth century, the war's outbreak in 1793 invested them with charged political and poetic meaning. In much of his poetry of the rest of the decade, Wordsworth portrayed a range of war's victims to illustrate what he termed the 'calamities … consequent upon war' ('Advertisement' to *Guilt and Sorrow*). Wordsworth's war poetry of the 1790s includes the following major works: *Salisbury Plain*, which tells the story of how a family are impoverished by war, leaving the father figure no option but to enlist, and forcing the rest of the family to follow him abroad, joining with 'the brood / That lap, their very nourishment, their brother's blood' [314–5];

'The Discharged Soldier', which describes the poet's unsettling encounter with a ghostly, skeletal soldier returned from the West Indies; 'The Ruined Cottage', with its moving depiction of Margaret's descent into madness after her husband has enlisted; and the *Lyrical Ballad* 'Old Man Travelling', with its heart-breaking description of an ageing father's journey to bid farewell to his dying son who has been fatally wounded in a sea battle.

This focus on the victims of conflict in the 1790s was politically controversial; one reviewer wrote of 'Old Man Travelling' that it seemed 'pointed against the war'.[5] As a writer who described the sufferings caused by war, Wordsworth came close to fulfilling the role of the 'Jacobin Poet', a target of attack for *The Anti-Jacobin*. According to this loyalist newspaper, founded in 1797 by future prime minister George Canning, poetry represented one of the most dangerous forms of 'Jacobinism', by which it meant sympathy for the French cause or support for the principles of the revolution. In its very first issue, *The Anti-Jacobin* argued that the poetic scene was dominated by the anti-war and pro-Gallic verses of the 'Jacobin Poet' and it outlined the differences between such verse and that of the loyal 'Old Poet'. Whereas the loyalist poet 'was a Warrior, at least in imagination; and sung the actions of the Heroes of his Country, in strains which "made Ambition Virtue," and which overwhelmed the horrors of War in its glory', in the work of the 'Jacobin Poet' 'we are presented with nothing but contusions and amputations, plundered peasants and deserted looms.'[6] The major targets for such attacks were Wordsworth's friends and fellow 'Lake Poets' Robert Southey and Samuel Taylor Coleridge, as is illustrated by James Gillray's brilliant visual satires on 'Jacobin' writing, 'The Friend of Humanity and the Knife-Grinder', which ridicules Southey's humanitarian poetry, and 'The New Morality', which presents the two poets with asses' heads. Southey's poetry was even more 'pointed against the war' than Wordsworth's, as is revealed by his poem 'The Sailor's Mother' from *Poems* (1799). This poem redeploys the structure of Wordsworth's 'Old Man Travelling', describing an encounter with a parent travelling to visit her injured child, in this case a sailor who has been press-ganged into the navy and blinded in a sea battle by a French 'fire ball', 'some cursed thing / That bursts and burns', as the old woman describes it.[7]

Wordsworth's political allegiances and his literary response to the war began to transform around the turn of the century. In the space of less than a decade, the poet would move from being one of the potential targets of *The Anti-Jacobin* to inclusion within the pages of *The Anti-Gallican*, a popular anthology of patriotic and bellicose writings produced to encourage British resistance to the French invasion threat. This remarkable conversion to the anti-Gallican cause was in large part due to what Wordsworth saw as the changing nature of the conflict itself during these years. He later described the period between the French 'subjugation of Switzerland' in 1798 and the Peace of Amiens of 1802–3 as the time when the war with France became 'just and necessary' [*Prose Works* I, 226]. It was the French invasion of Switzerland that prompted Coleridge's poetic repudiation of the Gallic cause, as described in his 'France: an Ode' of 1798, a poem initially titled 'The Recantation: An Ode'. This French military aggression towards a country that was seen by many in Britain as the home of liberty (an idea found in Wordsworth's sonnet 'Two Voices are there') was one indication of the shift in the nation's military policy. As Wordsworth wrote in *The Prelude*, Frenchmen had 'become oppressors in their turn', changing 'a war of self-defence / For one of conquest, losing sight of all / Which they had struggled for' [*Prelude* X, 791–4].

Wordsworth's anxieties about this shift in French military policy from self-defence to conquest were further exacerbated by the rise of Napoleon Bonaparte, the Corsican general who seized power as First Consul in 1799 and became Consul for Life in 1802. Wordsworth's initial reaction to Napoleon is hard to determine, unlike those of Coleridge and Southey, who for a brief period had cherished high hopes of a figure whom they hoped might rejuvenate the cause of Liberty. Ultimately, however, Wordsworth would come to see 'the catastrophe' of Napoleon's coronation in 1805 — when 'a Pope / Is summoned in, to crown an Emperor' — as enacting the final setting of the revolutionary sun that had risen in such splendour. Like 'the dog / Returning to his vomit', with Napoleon's coronation France had returned to absolutism [*Prelude* X, 930–40]. (See fig. 6 for James Gillray's contemporary satire of Napoleon's coronation and fig. 7 for the manuscript of this crucial passage of *The Prelude*.)

The brief respite in hostilities of the Peace of Amiens of 1802–3 was enormously important for Wordsworth, both politically and personally. Politically, it marked the moment when the war against France became 'just and necessary', due to the consolidation of Napoleon's power and the increasingly militaristic nature of his regime. Personally, it enabled Wordsworth to return to France for the first time in a decade and to seek to resolve one of the most difficult issues in his own private life. During his time in France in 1791, the young poet had met and fallen in love with Annette Vallon, but for financial reasons he had been forced to return to England

Figure 6. James Gillray (1756–1815), *The Grand Coronation Procession of Napoleone the 1st, Emperor of France, from the Church of Notre Dame, Decr 2d 1804*, 1805.

© Trustees of the British Museum.

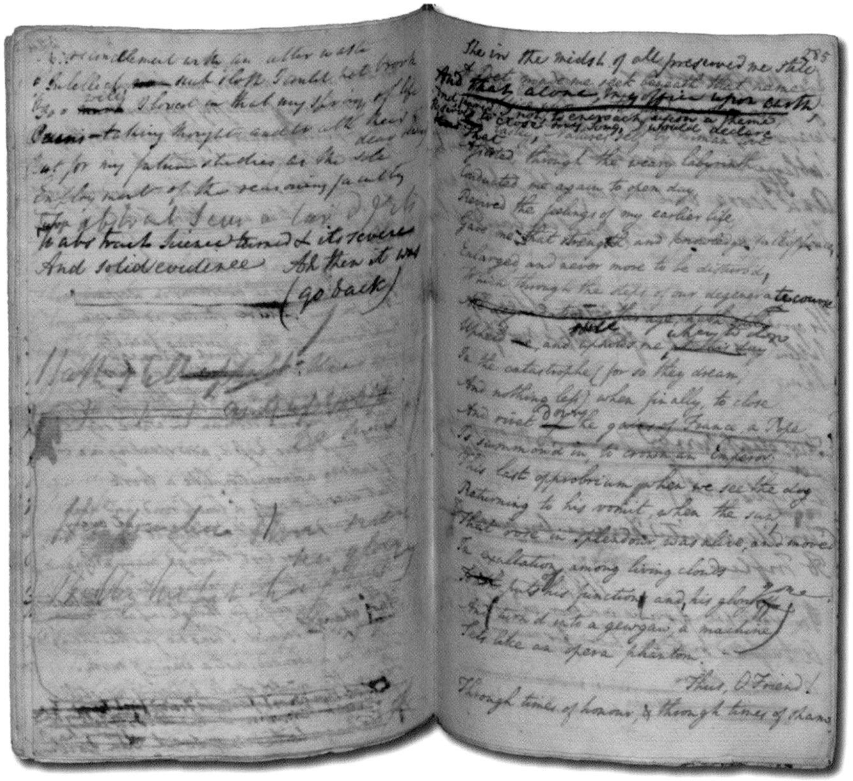

Figure 7. William Wordsworth (1770–1850), *The Prelude*, Book X, 1805, lines 919–42.

in 1792, having left behind Annette who was pregnant with his child. The outbreak of war the following year prevented Wordsworth from returning to France as he intended. It was not until 1802 that the poet was able to travel to France, meeting Annette and daughter Caroline at Calais and informing them of his intention to marry his childhood friend Mary Hutchinson. Little is known about this meeting. Much of Wordsworth's poetry of the trip focuses instead on the contrast between the Revolutionary France of the previous decade, when Wordsworth witnessed the 'festivals of new-born Liberty', and its current condition under Napoleon, by which time the designation 'Citizen' has become 'a hollow word, / As if a dead Man spake it!' ['To a Friend, Composed near Calais'].

Following the collapse of the Peace of Amiens in 1803, Napoleon established a vast army on the north coast of France intent on invading Britain; 'Impatient to put out the only light / Of Liberty that yet remains on Earth!', as Wordsworth put it in one of his many invasion poems ['October, 1803']. As described by Richard Matlak in his essay in this volume, Wordsworth himself participated in the remarkable British response to this invasion threat, enrolling in the Grasmere Volunteers in October 1803. Later that month, Dorothy wrote of her brother that 'surely there was never a more determined hater of the French nor one more willing to do his utmost to destroy them if they really do come' [letter to Catherine Clarkson 9 Oct 1803]. Wordsworth turned to poetry as a means of further participating in the conflict. In April 1802, he had rediscovered the sonnet form, taking fire when Dorothy had read him Milton's sonnets. Now, in this moment of crisis, when the nation needed to unite against the enemy, Wordsworth assumed the Miltonic role, using the sonnet to stiffen the resolve of those who faced the invasion force. He sought through his writing to unite the nation, as he emphasizes in his 'Lines on the Expected Invasion. 1803':

> Come ye — whate'er your creed — O waken all,
> Whate'er your temper, at your Country's call;
> Resolving (this free-born Nation can)
> To have one Soul, and perish to a man,
> Or save this honoured Land from every Lord
> But British Reason and the British Sword. [15–20]

For Wordsworth, poetry was a crucial part of the war effort, and he submitted a number of his sonnets for publication in the daily newspaper *The Morning Post*. Others also recognized the role the poet's verse could play in the conflict. His highly Miltonic sonnet 'Anticipation', with its stirring imagining of French defeat and subsequent British celebration, was incorporated in 1804 into *The Anti-Gallican*, a volume dedicated to 'The Volunteers of the United Kingdom, who with an impulse of genuine patriotism, have offered their services to defend the Rights of their Country, from the Violation threatened by an implacable foe.'[8]

Wordsworth's determined contribution to the war effort, as both a volunteer and a poet, highlights an element of his writing and personality that is often overlooked — its martial quality. While his work of the 1790s was forcefully anti-war, the poet nevertheless found excitement in battle and conflict. According to one source, in later life Wordsworth recalled that 'He had studied military history with great interest, and the strategy of war; and he always fancied that he had talents for command'.[9] Wordsworth gives fullest expression to his martial instincts in his poem 'Home at Grasmere' of 1800, where he describes how he swells 'with like desire' on hearing tales of courageous acts by 'one … / Or by a resolute few, who for the sake / Of glory fronted multitudes in arms' [923–8]. The poet goes on to describe how he experiences this martial 'desire' even when reading the regular reports of naval battle in the current war:

> I cannot at this moment read a tale
> Of two brave Vessels matched in deadly fight
> And fighting to the death, but I am pleased
> More than a wise Man ought to be; I wish,
> I burn, I struggle, and in soul am there. [929–33]

Wordsworth's interest in naval conflict and in the potentially heroic roles it offered are evident in much of his poetry of the first decade of the nineteenth century, from *Benjamin the Waggoner*, with its old sailor's re-enactment of the Battle of the Nile complete with model ship, to 'The Happy Warrior', written upon hearing the news of the death of Lord Nelson at Trafalgar. Paul Betz discusses Wordsworth's response to Nelson in greater detail in his essay in this volume. More generally, a sense of martial bellicosity underlies Wordsworth's most important definitions of power in *The Prelude*, from his experience on the summit of Snowdon, when he climbed the mountain 'as if in opposition set / Against an enemy', to the revelation inspired by the crossing of the Simplon pass, in which the mind is described as operating 'beneath … banners militant' [*Prelude* XIII, 30–1; VI, 543]. In these key passages, Wordsworth's experiences of wartime life inform his ideas of the imagination.

As the war with France progressed, Wordsworth increasingly defined the imagination as the most important site of conflict. He wrote his political tract *The Convention of Cintra* in 1809 in response to the British failure to push home an advantage in the early stages of the Peninsular War (see fig. 8 for Gillray's representation of this conflict). Wordsworth became obsessed with the writing of this prose pamphlet, in which he maintained that Napoleon's power was strongest 'in the imaginations of men, which are sure to fall under the bondage of long-continued success' [I, 249]. In fighting against France in the Iberian Peninsula, he insisted, 'We combated for victory in the empire of reason, for strong-holds in the imagination' [261]. And Wordsworth saw his own writing as playing a role within this imaginative combat. He published two parts of *The Convention of Cintra* in *The Courier* in December 1808 and January 1809 'for the sake of immediate and wide circulation' [*MY* I, 278], before the pamphlet itself was published in May 1809. Similarly, Wordsworth continued his poetic contribution to the war effort. Having collected together his verse writings on the war as 'Sonnets Dedicated to Liberty' in *Poems, in Two Volumes* (1807), he wrote thirty-two more sonnets on the European conflict between 1807 and 1813 and turned again to the form for his first poetic responses to Waterloo.

The Battle of Waterloo was a key moment in the literature of British Romanticism, as well as in European history. However, it was an event that the writers themselves battled over, adopting different sides and aligning themselves with the different protagonists, Wellington and Napoleon. The battle stimulated an extraordinary outpouring of verse. As the literary critic Francis Jeffrey commented, 'All our bards … great and small, and of all sexes, ages, and professions, from Scott and Southey down to hundreds without names or additions, have adventured upon this theme [of Waterloo]'.[10] As Jeffrey indicates, Walter Scott and Robert Southey were two of the 'great bards' who wrote poems about the battle, celebrating the victory in *The Field of Waterloo* and *The Poet's Pilgrimage to Waterloo* respectively. For them, Wellington was very much the battle's hero, and they both sought to answer the poetic challenge laid down by the popular versifier William Thomas Fitzgerald in his poem 'The Battle of Waterloo':

> But where's the BARD, however grac'd his name,
> Can venture to describe GREAT WELLESLEY's fame?
> Such Bard, in strength and loftiness of lays,
> May soar beneath hyperbole of praise,
> And yet not give the tribute that is due
> To BRITONS, WELLINGTON, led on by you!!
> For to the plains of WATERLOO belong
> The magic numbers of immortal song.

As these lines suggest, eulogistic praise of Wellington was a standard feature of the huge number of poems published on Waterloo.

Figure 8. James Gillray (1756–1815), *Spanish-Patriots attacking the French-Banditti. — Loyal Britons Lending a lift*, 1808. © Trustees of the British Museum.

Both Scott and Southey felt that it was essential for them to make the 'pilgrimage' to the scene of the battle. Waterloo rapidly became a tourist site and a place of inspiration for writers and artists, including J.M.W. Turner, whose visit to the battlefield and stunning painting *The Field of Waterloo* are discussed by David Blayney Brown in his essay in this volume. In 1816, Lord Byron rode across the battlefield as he travelled in self-imposed exile from Britain to Italy. Byron felt a strong affinity with Napoleon — he later described himself as 'The grand Napoleon of the realms of rhyme' [*Don Juan* Canto XI, stanza 55] — and for him the battle marked the final defeat of any remaining hopes for the French Revolution, as it did for William Hazlitt, who described Waterloo as the 'most fatal [battle] in all its consequences that was ever fought in the world'.[11] Byron saw Waterloo as the 'Crowning carnage' [*The Vision of Judgement* 38], the culmination of two decades of slaughter that had resulted in the restoration of monarchs to their thrones across Europe. In his most sustained poetic treatment of the battle in Canto III of *Childe Harold's Pilgrimage*, Byron even neglected to include the standard and expected praise of the Duke of Wellington (in a later unpublished stanza of *Don Juan*, he would go as far as to address the Duke as 'the best of cut-throats' [IX, 4]. In *Childe Harold*, Byron used Waterloo as the starting point for a complex, ambivalent and politically controversial analysis of Napoleon's character: 'There sank the greatest, nor the worst of men …' [Canto III, stanza 36].

Unlike Scott, Southey and Byron, Wordsworth did not visit Waterloo in the immediate aftermath of the combat. Rather, his major poetic response to the battle, the 'Ode. The Morning of the Day Appointed for a General Thanksgiving. January 18, 1816', was inspired by his 'feelings as collected in force upon the morning of the day appointed for a general Thanksgiving' [to John Scott 11 March 1816, *MY* II, 284]. Exchanging the sonnet form for the more elevated tones of the Ode, Wordsworth treated Waterloo in grand terms rather than giving the details of the battle as other poets did. For him, the battle needed to be understood as a divine event, a developing conception of the war with France that he had drawn on in the *Cintra* pamphlet, in which he presented the conflict as a struggle between good and evil, of the 'noblest services of light' against the Satanic figure of Napoleon [*Prose Works* I, 301]. Writing at the time of the national thanksgiving, Wordsworth argues that Napoleon's defeat at Waterloo must be understood primarily not as a British victory, but as an act of 'Almighty God':

> … one brief day is rightly set apart
> To Him who lifteth up and layeth low;
> For that Almighty God to whom we owe,
> Say not that we have vanquished — but that we survive.
>
> ['Thanksgiving Ode' 88–91]

Wordsworth investigates the full implications of his divine understanding of Waterloo in the Ode's most controversial lines (analysed in detail by Philip Shaw in his essay in this volume):

> We bow our heads before Thee, and we laud
> And magnify thy name, Almighty God!

But thy most dreadful instrument,

In working out a pure intent,

Is Man — arrayed for mutual slaughter, —

Yea, Carnage is thy daughter. [279–82]

These lines shocked Shelley, Hazlitt and Byron, who frequently invoked them as part of their post-Waterloo attacks on Wordsworth as a poet whom they saw as having deserted the cause of Liberty. For Wordsworth, they were the necessary if challenging implication of the way in which he had come to understand the war as part of a divine plan, akin to natural disasters. For him, it is God who is to be thanked for the ultimate defeat of Napoleon:

To thee — To thee —

On this appointed Day shall thanks ascend,

That Thou hast brought our warfare to an end,

And that we need no further victory! [289–92]

It was with some justification, then, that in his 'Thanksgiving Ode' Wordsworth presented the Battle of Waterloo as the moment when the 'Imagination' was 'satisfied'. Twenty-two years of war with France had helped shape the poet's imagination, making Waterloo the culmination of a poetic career that was still in its early stages when the conflict began. Though Wordsworth began this career as an anti-war poet, he increasingly came to see himself as actively engaged in the conflict through his writing, combating for victory in the empire of reason, for strongholds in the imagination. As the poet commented in the year after Waterloo, 'My whole soul was with those who were resolved to fight it out with Bonaparte' [to Henry Crabb Robinson 2 Aug 1816]. Wordsworth was a great writer of war poetry whose personal history and poetic development were shaped by the age of conflict in which he lived.

One remarkable testimony to the war's lasting legacy for the writers and artists who lived through it is Benjamin Robert Haydon's famous portrait of Wordsworth on Helvellyn, painted in 1842 (see fig. 4). Viewed out of context, this great portrait appears to be an archetypal representation of Wordsworth as poet removed from any historical or political concerns. By locating Wordsworth on the side of Helvellyn, Haydon associates the poet with the sublimity of the mountainous landscape that he celebrated in his writing, while his representation of Wordsworth's reflective pose, crossed arms and closed eyes suggests the poet is experiencing the sort of vision on the 'inward eye' that is celebrated as 'the bliss of solitude' in 'I Wandered Lonely as a Cloud'. However, during the climb of Helvellyn that this painting commemorates, Wordsworth was not thinking of mountains or daffodils, but of Wellington and Waterloo. Haydon's portrait commemorates the poet's last ascent of Helvellyn in 1840, during which Wordsworth composed his sonnet 'On a Portrait of the Duke of Wellington, upon the Field of Waterloo, By Haydon'. The poet's son-in-law, Edward Quillinan, wrote of the climb, 'I wish you could have seen the Old Poet, seated from time to time, as we paused for breath, on a rock writing down his Waterloo Sonnet.' Haydon's portrait, then, is both a tribute and a mark of gratitude to the poet who had praised his own artwork. Indeed, Haydon draws in his representation of Wordsworth on two of his earlier portraits of the rival protagonists of Waterloo, *Napoleon Musing at St Helena* (see fig. 1), painted in 1830, and its companion piece, *Wellington Musing on the Field of Waterloo* (see fig. 2), of 1839. Wordsworth had written a sonnet on the first of these paintings in 1832, 'To B. R. Haydon, Esq. on Seeing his Picture of Napoleon Buonaparte on the Island of St. Helena', in which he described how Haydon presented Napoleon with 'arms folded', 'sole-standing high on the bare hill'. These were elements that Haydon would redeploy in his painting of Wellington and then, of course, of Wordsworth himself, sole-standing high on Helvellyn. What this fascinating sequence of artistic tributes reveals is that in his portrait of Wordsworth, Haydon was drawing on the same iconographic tradition that he had used for Napoleon and Wellington. In doing so, Haydon equated the poet with the warriors and granted Wordsworth the same grand status as that held by the two major historical figures of the first half of the nineteenth century, the victor and the vanquished of Waterloo.

Abbreviations:

MY I: *Letters of William and Dorothy Wordsworth, The Middle Years, Part I, 1806–1811*, ed. E. de Selincourt, 2nd ed., revised by Mary Moorman (Oxford: Clarendon Press, 1967)

MY II: *Letters of William and Dorothy Wordsworth, The Middle Years, Part II, 1812–1820*, ed. E. de Selincourt, 2nd ed., revised by Mary Moorman and Alan G. Hill (Oxford: Clarendon Press, 1967)

Prose Works: William Wordsworth, *The Prose Works of William Wordsworth*, ed. W.J.B. Owen and Jane Worthington Smyser, 3 volumes (Oxford: Clarendon Press, 1974)

(Endnotes)

1. Robert Southey to Grosvenor Charles Bedford, 22 Aug 1815, *The Collected Letters of Robert Southey, Part Four: 1810–1815*, ed. Ian Packer and Lynda Pratt, http://www.rc.umd.edu/editions/southey_letters/Part_Four/HTML/letterEEd.26.2648.html

2. See Simon Bainbridge, *British Poetry and the Revolutionary and Napoleonic Wars: Visions of Conflict* (Oxford: Oxford University Press, 2003), 6

3. The poem's full title is 'Ode. The Morning of the Day Appointed for a General Thanksgiving. January 18, 1816'

4. All references to *The Prelude* are to the 1805 version as presented in *The Fourteen-Book Prelude*, ed. W. J. B. Owen (Ithaca, New York: Cornell University Press, 1985)

5. Dr Charles Burney, *Monthly Review*, xxix (June 1799), 202–10

6. *The Anti-Jacobin*, 20 Nov 1797, 12–14

7. Robert Southey, *Poems: The Second Volume* (Bristol: T.N. Longman and O. Rees, 1799), 206–15

8. *The Anti-Gallican, or, Standard of British Loyalty, Religion, and Liberty* (London: Vernor and Hood, and J. Asperne, 1804)

9. *The Prose Works of William Wordsworth*, ed. Alexander B. Grosart, 3 vols. (London: Edward Moxon, 1876), III, 451–2

10. Francis Jeffrey, *The Edinburgh Review*, 54 (December 1816), 295

11. *The Complete Works of William Hazlitt*, ed. P.P. Howe, 21 vols. (London: J.M. Dent, 1930–34), XV, 269

Saturday 28th November.

A very fine sunny morning. Soldiers still going by — I should have mentioned that yesterday when we went with Wm to Mr Luff's we met a soldier & his wife, he with a child in his arms, she carrying a bundle & his gun — we gave them some halfpence it was such a pretty sight.

Dorothy Wordsworth's Grasmere journal, 28 November 1801

DOROTHY WORDSWORTH & THE IMPACT OF WAR

PAMELA WOOF

'SURELY IT MIGHT seem', wrote Dorothy Wordsworth in April 1814 after hearing the decrees of the Congress of Vienna, 'that to us, encircled by these mountains, our own little concerns outweigh the mighty joys and sorrows of nations'. 'It is not so', she goes on:

> — every heart has exulted — we have danced for
> joy! But how strange! it is like a dream — peace
> peace — all in a moment — prisoners let loose
> — Englishmen and Frenchmen brothers at once!
> — no treaties — no stipulations. [24 April 1814][1]

Dorothy felt the joy; her exclamations indicate it. She was in her mid-forties and had lived for more than twenty years, all her adult life so far, with the consciousness of war. This peace in 1814 that gave her such ecstasy lasted scarcely a year. Napoleon, exiled to Elba, returned to France, and Dorothy's anxiety likewise returned until after the victory of Waterloo in June 1815.

She had had an awareness of threat for so long; at nineteen, and living in her guardian Uncle William's rectory in the quiet village of Forncett in Norfolk, she had feared for her younger brother John, an adolescent midshipman in the East India Fleet. War with Spain was entirely possible and merchant vessels had to have a substantial convoy of warships. John was forever on the high seas: 'from Whitehaven he will sail to the West Indies or America, and next spring he goes out again to the East', wrote Dorothy in spring 1792, when at the same time she was voicing concern for her elder brother's safety: 'William is still in France, and I begin to wish he was in England; he assures me however that he is perfectly safe, but as we hear daily accounts of Insurrections and Broils I cannot be quite easy; though I think he is wise enough to get out of the way of Danger' [8 May 1792]. Wordsworth was still in France in mid-October, but by Christmas 1792 he was safely in London. With the execution of Louis XVI in January 1793 the tension hardened into open war, and this lasted, with short breaks in 1802 and 1814, until after Waterloo in June 1815.

When Dorothy, now twenty-two, left Forncett Rectory and her uncle's protection in 1794, and chose to experience the world alongside her brother, she

Figure 9. Amos Green (1735–1807), *Dove Cottage*, date unknown.

moved nearer to realising the effects of war. At first this was at no profound level: 'Do you intend to pay the powder tax?', she asked her old friend Jane Pollard,

> It has been much the subject of conversation in
> all parties at Newcastle, and no doubt at Halifax
> and everywhere else ... every individual however
> [insig]nificant should avail himself of every fair
> opportunity of declaring his disapprobation of
> the present destructive war ...
> [mid-April 1795]

Powdered hair in fact fell out of fashion and Prime Minister William Pitt's war tax on powder dwindled away. Rural communities had more basic problems: Dorothy noticed how the peasants around Racedown in Dorset, where she was living with her brother, were 'miserably poor' [30 Nov 1795], but it was not till she had lived longer with her politically reformist brother and been in the company of the zealous, agitating Coleridge that she came nearer to the realisation that war directly affected seemingly remote individuals, particularly those from the poorest ranks. In her primarily landscape-seascape-skyscape descriptive Alfoxden journal, written in Somerset in the first few months of 1798, there is only one entry describing a stranger encountered on the roads, only one:

> ... the moon and two planets; sharp and frosty.
> Met a razor-grinder with a soldier's jacket on, a
> Knapsack upon his back, and a boy to drag his
> wheel. The sea very black, and making a loud
> noise as we came through the wood, loud as if
> disturbed, and the wind was silent.
> [DWJ 22 Feb 1798][2]

Clearly the man with his red jacket had been in the war and was now attempting to survive. Sky, sea, sound and silence interest Dorothy more than conversation with the man (if any) or his story. It would not be until Dorothy walked the roads in Grasmere in 1800 that the people who were the wretched detritus of war spoke as individual suffering human beings to her, told their stories, and touched her compassion.

Meanwhile for Dorothy there was travel to Germany (war prohibited any movement into France), learning the language, and settling down as companion and scribe for Wordsworth as he composed magnificently during the icy confinement of the Goslar winter, 1798–9; all this occupied Dorothy. 'If the state of Europe will permit', she had announced before they left England, 'we shall endeavour to get into Switzerland' [to Mrs Rawson, Dorothy's 'aunt', in Halifax 13 June/3 July 1798]. But she and Wordsworth were back in England in April 1799 and in their first true home together in Grasmere by late December. (See fig. 9 for Amos Green's contemporaneous drawing of their home at Town End.) Beggars were commonplace on the roads: some called at the house; others paused in their journeying and told their stories on the road. Dorothy, either walking alone or with Wordsworth, listened. She not only gave charities of bread or small coins that kept people going: she gave her attention; she listened. In her journal she often recounted the sad circumstances of poverty and the strengths of human resilience. This was clearly of interest to both brother and sister, for the essay or Preface that accompanies the second edition of *Lyrical Ballads*, 1800, came clearly out of conversation between them, and Dorothy, by now, was entirely sympathetic to her brother's radical endeavour to promote sympathy and understanding of the poor among the nation's middle-class readers. Those readers must be encouraged to feel that we have all of us one human heart.

The long war that Dorothy Wordsworth lived through created poverty both directly and indirectly. There is the man who called 'in a soldiers dress — he was thirty years old — of Cockermouth, had lost a leg & thigh in battle was going to his home. He could earn more money in travelling with his ass than at home' [DWJ 9 Oct 1800]. A 'broken soldier' who called could only beg; two soldiers together became drunk [DWJ 1 Dec 1801]; another was with his wife, 'he with a child in his arms, she carrying a bundle & his gun' [DWJ 28 Nov 1801] (see fig. 10 for the manuscript page of Dorothy's journal); an old man called,

> a grey-headed man, above 70 years of age; he said
> he had been a soldier, that his wife & children
> had died in Jamaica ... I talked a while to him, a
> woman called travelling to Glasgow.
> [DWJ 2 June 1802]

There were young men, old men, soldiers and sailors, all walking, hoping to find a harbour, perhaps in their native parishes.

And there were women. The indirect effects of war fell heavily on women: trade embargoes on importing grain, for instance, meant that farmers had to grow more; more fields were enclosed; there was less common land; prices went up; agricultural and industrial 'improvements' put people out of work; they went to the towns to hard mechanised labour. 'A poor girl called to beg', wrote Dorothy, 'who had no work at home & was going in search of it to Kendal' [DWJ 9 June 1800]. The plucky Cockermouth traveller has been 'over the mountains these thirty years' with her threads and hardware [DWJ 10 Oct 1800]. But most of the women Dorothy talks to do not survive so well. Another Cockermouth woman with two little girls was going after her husband who had left her for another woman. The woman was in distress with anger, the children half-starved, and Dorothy, realising that she and the woman, both from Cockermouth, were the same age, thirty, gave her a shilling, 'I believe 6^d more than I ought to have given' [DWJ 4 May 1802]. One woman had been an officer's wife, had had a muslin gown — like Dorothy's; they had been in the West Indies; he had been shot; her second husband was also wounded and was now limping ahead of her trying to get to Whitehaven [DWJ 27 Nov 1801].

There are children too: the pretty little boy, hardly grown in the two years since Dorothy had seen him, wearing the same ragged drab coat and still quietly hungry [DWJ 12 Feb 1802]; a little girl, about four, 'half-starved' and wearing 'a pair of slippers that had belonged to some gentleman's child, down at the heels, but it was not easy to keep them on ...' [DWJ 4 May 1802]. As in Wordsworth's 'Ruined

'Saturday 28th November. — A very fine sunny morning. Soldiers still going by — I should have mentioned that yesterday when we went with Wm to Mr Luff's we met a soldier & his wife, he with a child in his arms, she carrying a bundle & his gun — we gave them some halfpence it was such a pretty sight.'

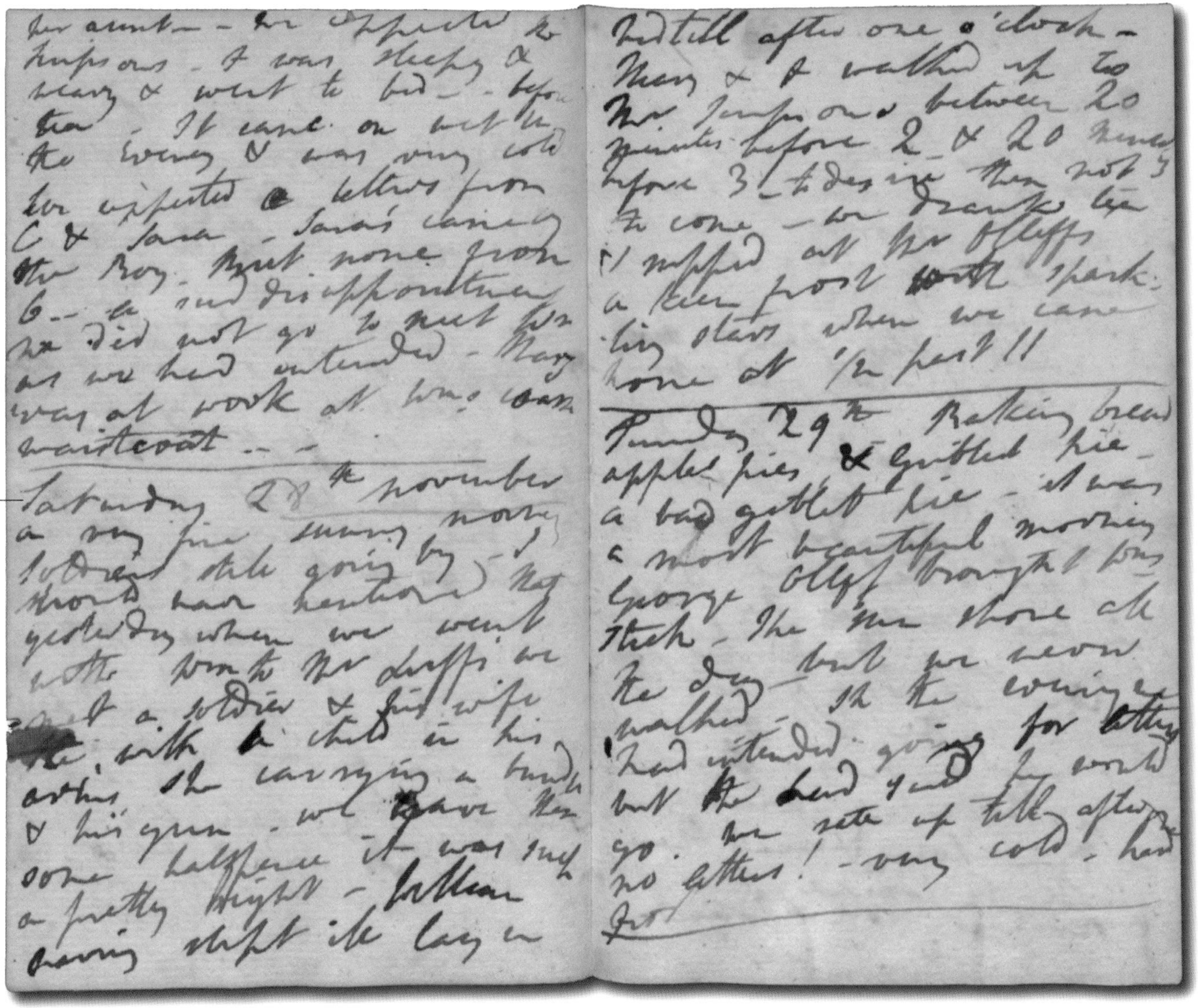

Figure 10. Dorothy Wordsworth (1771–1855), Grasmere journal, 28 November 1801.

Cottage' (1797) the poverty that comes with war and with agricultural hardship hits the women and the children, hits the whole family. As Dorothy says, as an added thought in her journal, and thinking of the poor woman, the little boy, the husband with his leg wounded by a slate torn by wind from the roof of their half-ruined hovel, 'this woman's was but a *common* case' [DWJ 12 Feb 1802]. At night, hearing 'the dismal sound of a crying infant' Dorothy went to the window of their Grasmere cottage and, with the snow still lying on the ground, 'had light enough to see that a man was driving a cart which seemed not to be very full, & that a woman with an infant in her arms was following close behind & a dog close to her. It was a wild & melancholy sight' [DWJ 12 Feb 1802]. Indeed, it was. Dorothy's comment is just, and the picture she presents is symbolic of the hardship that comes to the ordinary poor in a time of war. They are so many and so commonplace that even Dorothy, sympathising, can hardly encounter them all as individual social beings like herself. Poverty envelops them; they are, with only one exception, nameless in the journal, almost objects to her in her pity as she meets them on the road.

The better-off, of course, fared better; they could flourish, while Dorothy's good yet impoverished neighbours, the Ashburners, had been forced to sell their land. Gradually in Grasmere valley small holders of property, [e]statesmen, were being bought out; the fewer farms became bigger, more economic, more powerful. But Peggy Ashburner grieved, remembering, Dorothy reported in her journal, how the bit of earth that the Ashburners had formerly owned and loved had been for Peggy something essential:

She said she used to take such pleasure in the cattle & sheep — 'O how pleased I used to be when they fetched them down, & when I had been a bit poorly I would gang out upon a hill & look ower t'fields & see them & it used to do me so much good you cannot think.'
[DWJ 24 Nov 1801]

Though war's distress fell most upon the poor, its tentacles were universally noticeable: in children, for example, those who were not starving, and who lived in valleys far from the action; and also in adults involved in the private concerns of their own lives. In the middle of March 1802 Dorothy Wordsworth in Grasmere recorded talking with her brother one morning at breakfast. They talked about butterflies and how in childhood (much of it spent apart from each other) their experiences differed: 'I used to chase them a little', wrote Dorothy, but,

I was afraid of brushing the dust off their wings & did not catch them — He told me how they used to kill all the white ones when he went to school because they were frenchmen.
[DWJ 14 March 1802]

So Wordsworth and his fellow Hawkshead schoolboys acted out the war in pacific nature's midst. And Wordsworth as an adult, over the years, throughout the war, keeping and losing, losing and keeping his radical ideas, both loved and hated the French, seeing them at times as the white butterflies of his school days. Further, in war, public affairs could interrupt private relationships. Trying to keep in contact with Annette Vallon, whom he had loved in France in 1792, and who was the mother of his child, was only spasmodically possible. Most letters simply did not arrive. 'William has had a letter from France since we came here', wrote Dorothy from Racedown to her old friend Jane Marshall, in November 1795. 'Annette mentions having despatched half a dozen none of which he has received' [30 Nov 1795]. Only after seven more years was there a truce in the war and letters then reached Grasmere. Both Wordsworth and Dorothy wrote to Annette in 1802. This was preparatory to their meeting her in Calais and Wordsworth's making a settlement for her and his child Caroline; he then returned to England for his marriage to Mary Hutchinson.

But war's tentacles could stretch further: they could create anxieties in Grasmere other than those connected with rural economics or private relationships. In 1803 Dorothy was again 'exceedingly anxious to hear something about John', she told her brother Richard in May 1803:

> We have been uneasy about him on account of the pressing of men; we were afraid his ship might lose her crew: and John be detained on that account, and now that the War is certain we are still more anxious to know whether he has sailed or not ... I cannot express how very anxious I am about him. [22 May 1803]

The war was back; the 1802 Peace of Amiens was over, the English Channel again dangerous and poor men would still accept the King's shilling or be pressed into the army; some would return to walk such roads as the one through Grasmere.

Meanwhile, in August and September 1803, Dorothy and Wordsworth — and Coleridge with them for some of the time — walked, though for pleasure, not need, the roads of Scotland. They had a horse and an 'Irish jaunting car' to help; this brought its own anxiety. And France was far from forgotten. As English travellers in Scotland they very occasionally met with an inn landlady's refusal to house them despite there being room [*Journals* 6–7 Sept 1803, I, 348–54].[3] The landscape, however, always pleased: 'Wherever we looked, it was a delightful feeling that there was something beyond' [*Journals* 25 Aug 1803, I, 253], but the reader is less sure of the accuracy of Dorothy's social understanding:

> In talking of the French and the present times, their language was what most people would call Jacobinical. They spoke much of the oppressions endured by the Highlanders further up, of the absolute impossibility of their living in any comfort, and of the cruelty of laying so many

restraints on emigration. Then they spoke with animation of the attachment of the clans to their lairds: 'The laird of this place, Glengyle, could have commanded so many men who would have followed him to the death, and now there are none left.' [*Journals* 27 Aug 1803, I, 267–8]

Soon Wordsworth and Dorothy came to the pass of Killicrankie, its battle 'famous', as Dorothy says, 'in military history', and she connects the surge of Highland loyalty for the Stuarts in 1689, heroically (and victoriously) pitted against the efficient English and Dutch forces of William and Mary, with the notion, impossible as it would be in 1803, that similar Highland loyalty might rise to aid the English against a feared Napoleonic attack:

> When we were travelling in Scotland an invasion was hourly looked for, and one could not but think with some regret of the times when from the now depopulated Highlands forty or fifty thousand men might have been poured down for the defence of the country, under such leaders as the Marquis of Montrose ...
> [*Journals* 8 Sept 1803, I, 356]

A fanciful and hypothetical analysis, but it indicates the real anxiety about the possibility of invasion. Wordsworth wrote a sonnet on the idea[4] and joined the Grasmere Volunteers immediately on his return: 'our Grasmere Volunteers do walk past the door twice a week in their Red Coats to be exercised at Ambleside', wrote Dorothy, but Wordsworth had not been called upon to exercise, and, she declared, 'we have given over even thinking about invasion' [15 Jan 1804].

For a few years anxiety in Grasmere was focused on the sea. John's death and the sinking of his ship, the *Earl of Abergavenny*, in February 1805 was not a calamity of war, but it immeasurably heightened Dorothy's sense of the dangers of the sea. Coleridge, returning, it was thought, from Malta, became a worry:

> What a sad event for us is the Capture of the Malta Fleet! We may however be thankful that Coleridge himself was not with it. [to Lady Beaumont 18 March 1805]

The 'great Battle', as Dorothy called it, that year was of course Trafalgar in October 1805. It had been immediately preceded by the capitulation to Napoleon of yet another city, Ulm, and Dorothy, left alone in Grasmere with little John and baby Dora (William and Mary were visiting Mary's brother near Penrith), felt

> quite overwhelmed with the disastrous tidings contained in three newspapers which I received at one time while they were absent, and read over

by my solitary fire-side till I could not endure the pain of my own thoughts ...

'What a contrast in the silence of the air, the clear sky, and the peacefully decaying trees to the turbulence of men!', she continued in her letter of 4 November 1805 to Lady Beaumont. Wordsworth, returning from the family visit, waited for more recent newspapers in Ambleside, but there were no 'authentic details of the event of the great Battle. There was nothing but a confirmation of the general belief that it was as bad as possible' [4 Nov 1805]. It was not until the following week, 10 November, that the Wordsworths heard certain news of Trafalgar. Now it was Mary who was at home with the children, and Wordsworth and Dorothy were taking a short pedestrian excursion along the shores of Ullswater. Dorothy began her Ullswater journal entry for 10 November 1805 with the joyful, and troubling, news about the great naval battle that had taken place on 21 October:

> November 10th, Saturday. A beautiful sunny morning. When we were at breakfast heard the tidings of Lord Nelson's death and the victory of Trafalgar. Went to the inn to make further inquiries. I was shocked to hear that there had been great rejoicings at Penrith. Returned by William's rock and grove ... [*Journals* 10 Nov 1805, I, 419]

Towards the end of that November, a quiet night, the children in bed and Wordsworth and Mary again at Park House with Thomas Hutchinson, Dorothy writes to Lady Beaumont in more detail about her sorrows and anxieties — for her brother drowned in February 1805; for the wandering Coleridge, 'Heaven preserve him from Captivity in France!'; and for Nelson:

> ... the tidings of Lord Nelson's Fate reached us at Patterdale. We were at Breakfast when Mr Luff's Maid-servant opened the door, and, shewing only her head, with an uncouth stare and a grin of pleasure told us that there had been a great victory, and Lord Nelson was shot. It was a blow. I was not collected enough to doubt, and burst into tears; but William would not believe all at once, and forced me to suspend my grief till he had made further inquiries. At the Inn we were told that there were 'great rejoicings at Penrith — all the Bells ringing'. 'Then, I exclaimed, he cannot be dead!' but we soon heard enough to leave us without a doubt, and bitterly did we lament for him and our Country. [29 Nov 1805]

Silence from Coleridge continued for several months to mystify his friends: Dorothy was in an 'anxiety of expectation'. He was said to be coming from Trieste by way of Vienna, and Robert Southey was hoping he would get to Vienna before the French; 'he may be detained at Hamburgh after all by the freezing of the Elbe'; it was rumoured he was in Naples, and Dorothy feared storms at sea; could he 'accompany the Troops from Naples to Sicily?' He was heard of in Rome, 'Stoddart believed under a borrowed name'; he had been 'stopped by the French in Italy ...' [to Catherine Clarkson 14 Dec 1805; Lady Beaumont 19 Jan 1806, 2 March 1806; Wordsworth to Walter Scott 4 July 1806]. He reached England in August 1806, but did not catch up with the Wordsworths until the end of October.

Dorothy was not writing a daily journal, as she had from 1800 until early 1803; she was not listening and talking to the poor people who walked the roads. She was immersed in family: there were now three small children. They had all lived in the Hall Farmhouse in Coleorton, Leicestershire for a winter, 1806–7; they had moved to a larger Grasmere house, Allan Bank, in 1808, where a fourth child was born. Dorothy, as well as being her brother's best amanuensis, supervised both the childbirths and the house moves. And it was she who wrote the moving and compelling account in 1808 of the freak snow-storm deaths on local hills of the parents of a large poor family. Money in consequence was generously subscribed. Thoughts of war were not uppermost.

But 1808 brought the Peninsular War. Napoleon's invasion of Portugal was too much. As late as May 1809, Wordsworth 'made a resolution to write upon publick affairs in the *Courier*, or some other newspaper ... I do not much like the thought of it ...', wrote Dorothy to De Quincey [1 May 1809]. In the event, Wordsworth did not, like Coleridge, become a regular journalist, but for months he had been composing an impassioned prose pamphlet in defence of the right of nations to be free from unprovoked tyrannical invasion. His pamphlet on *The Convention of Cintra* was also a criticism of the British generals involved in the Peninsula; one of them was the brilliant, though young, Sir Arthur Wellesley, later Duke of Wellington. The generals had allowed, in Wordsworth's view, a weak, almost defeatist and unprincipled treaty to be made with the conquered French. Dorothy was aware of Wordsworth's strong emotion, of the fearful eagerness for news, the suspense of waiting, the passionate sense of patriotism, and the need to write, revise, correct, as information filtered to their remote northern valley. But she was not directly involved in helping Wordsworth with the writing of *Cintra*. Assistance was provided by the admiring young De Quincey, who stayed for two months at Allan Bank. That house, what with Wordsworth, De Quincey and *The Convention of Cintra*, and later Coleridge and *The Friend*, must have reverberated with ideas and moral passions.

Neither Dorothy nor Sara Hutchinson, who was also at Allan Bank, took seriously Wordsworth's at times genuine anxiety lest his writing get him into serious trouble with Government:

> We Females shall be very sorry to find that the
> pamphlet is not published for we have not the
> least fear of Newgate — if there was but a garden
> to walk in we think we should do very nicely ...
> [Sara Hutchinson to De Quincey 5 May 1809]

So wrote Sara Hutchinson on 5 May 1809, and on 6 May, the next day, Dorothy corroborated Sara's confidence. She commented to De Quincey, then in London,

> William still continues to haunt himself with
> fancies about Newgate and Dorchester, or some
> other gaol, but as his mind clings to the gloomy,
> Newgate is his favourite theme.

The war dragged on and Dorothy commented at the end of 1810,

> We are heartless respecting Wellington's doing
> much. Yet there *never* was a time of so much
> hope in the Spanish and Portuguese themselves.
> [30 Dec 1810]

Wellington, as history knows, would redeem everything in a few years. Coleridge, unlike the Wordsworths, retained all along his admiration for Wellesley; 'servile adulations', commented Dorothy, of Coleridge's essays in the *Courier*, and she grieved at 'the waste and prostitution of his [Coleridge's] fine genius' [16 June 1811]. Fortunately, in Dorothy's view, Napoleon too was losing credibility:

> God be thanked the tide is turned against
> Buonaparte and we shall see, I trust, the
> delusions speedily vanish which even in

England has spread too widely, that he was a
great genius and a great hero. [12 May 1811]

It was not until after Russia, until April 1814, that Napoleon had fallen so far that he abdicated and was exiled to Elba, with the consequent movement towards restoration of the Bourbon monarchy, peace in Europe, and Dorothy's expression of ecstatic joy with which this essay began. She wrote of her joy on 24 April 1814 and by October she was thinking tentatively of going to Paris with Sara Hutchinson, intending to assist at the arrangements for the wedding of her niece Caroline, for twelve years unvisited. Spring of 1815 was fixed for the wedding, with Wordsworth and Dorothy to attend. But Napoleon had not finished; he escaped from Elba. Again, as so often, war and political movements interrupted the private plans of individuals: Wordsworth and Dorothy could not go to Paris for Caroline's wedding.

Of course Dorothy's joy in the peace that came with the victory at Waterloo was renewed. But it was more cautious this time:

> I dare not hope that matters will not be again
> mismanaged. The joy of victory is indeed an awful
> thing, and I had no patience with the tinkling of
> our Ambleside bells.

And she had no patience with the Prince Regent's recommendation that 'further proofs of the munificence of the people should be shewn to the Duke of Wellington. It is perfectly childish to be in such a bustle.' She felt the gallant and killed Duke of Brunswick should have had the tribute of respectful tears [28 June 1815].

The general fascination with Napoleon continued to irritate Dorothy. In the middle of August 1815 she wrote to Catherine Clarkson,

Oh I am sick of the adulation, the folly, the idle Curiosity which was gathered together round the ship [the *Bellerophon* that was to take the defeated Napoleon to St Helena] that held the dastardly spirit that has so long been the scourge of all whom he *could* injure. *He* kill himself! No, he is too much of a coward ... but he is not worth talking about ...

She thought that the French people were equally deplorable: 'if left to themselves they would soon plague us and the rest of the world. Would that all the English had Prussian hearts ...' [15 Aug 1815].

The Wordsworths were by now living happily at Rydal Mount, a mile or two from Grasmere. Dorothy did not come close to the war again until the late summer of 1820. Then she saw Annette for the first time since 1802 and got to know Wordsworth's child, his now married daughter Caroline. She stood on the Field of Waterloo. Only now were all the personalities forgotten. Dorothy was conscious not of the individuals in the long drama of war but of a huge human sorrow that affected so many that it was like humanity at large, suffering amid the warm, growing beauty of an ever changing and ever present nature.

We stood upon grass, and corn fields where *heaps* of our countrymen lay buried beneath our feet. There was little to be seen; but much to be felt; — sorrow and sadness, and even something like horror breathed out of the ground as we stood upon it! ['Journals of a Tour on the Continent' 1820, *Journals* II, 29]

From a distance, for over twenty years, Dorothy Wordsworth had watched this long punishing war; the earth, the very ground of its final battlefield, emphasised for her not triumph, but horror.

(Endnotes)

1. Dates alone indicate letters, and texts of these will be found by date in *The Letters of William and Dorothy Wordsworth*, ed. E. de Selincourt; *The Early Years, 1787–1805*, rev. Chester L Shaver (Oxford: Oxford University Press, 1967); *The Middle Years, 1806–11*, rev. Mary Moorman (Oxford: Oxford University Press, 1969); *1812–20*, rev. Mary Moorman and Alan G. Hill (Oxford: Oxford University Press 1970). Letters quoted are written by Dorothy Wordsworth, unless otherwise indicated.

2. A date preceded by 'DWJ' indicates that the quotation will be found by date in *The Grasmere and Alfoxden Journals*, Oxford World's Classics, ed. Pamela Woof (Oxford: Oxford University Press, 2002)

3. A date preceded by '*Journals*' indicates that the quotation is from *The Journals of Dorothy Wordsworth*, ed. E. de Selincourt, 2 vols. (London: Macmillan, 1952)

4. 'Six thousand Veterans practised in War's game', sonnet written October 1803, published 1807.

Old Man Travelling; Animal Tranquillity and Decay, A Sketch (1798)
William Wordsworth

            The little hedge-row birds,
That peck along the road, regard him not.
He travels on, and in his face, his step,
His gait, is one expression; every limb,
His look and bending figure, all bespeak
A man who does not move with pain, but moves
With thought — He is insensibly subdued
To settled quiet: he is one by whom
All effort seems forgotten, one to whom
Long patience has such mild composure given,
That patience now doth seem a thing, of which
He hath no need. He is by nature led
To peace so perfect, that the young behold
With envy, what the old man hardly feels.
    — I asked him whither he was bound, and what
The object of his journey; he replied
'Sir! I am going many miles to take
A last leave of my son, a mariner,
Who from a sea-fight has been brought to Falmouth,
And there is dying in an hospital.'

'HER HOMELY TALE': THE WORDSWORTHS & WARTIME LIVES

JENNY UGLOW

❧

IN GRASMERE, IN November 1801, William and Dorothy Wordsworth met a soldier and his wife on the road, 'he with a child in his arms, she carrying a bundle & his gun — we gave them some halfpence it was such a pretty sight' [DWJ 28 Nov 1801].[1] The reversed picture is touching, the man with the child, the woman with the gun, and they were probably going home after the signing of preliminaries for the Peace of Amiens, a lull in the war. But all too soon the soldiers would march off again. Between 1793 and 1815 one in five families had men in the army or navy, militia or volunteers. Thousands of men died. The plight of those left behind is dramatized in Wordsworth's 'The Ruined Cottage', begun in the West Country in the late 1790s and revised during the early years at Grasmere.

For the rural poor, life was already difficult. When the Wordsworths moved to Racedown in Dorset in 1795, Dorothy was horrified. The peasants of the West Country were miserably poor, she told her friend Jane Marshall, 'indeed they are not at all beyond what might be expected in savage life' [30 Nov 1795].[2] Even in smart towns like Bath, where Wordsworth's fellow poet Robert Southey was living, working people suffered during the depression that followed the declaration of war:

plans for new crescents were stopped and builders lost work; local colliers, and even staymakers, went on strike. There was tension here too, as in many other towns, between loyalist supporters of Prime Minister William Pitt and the war and radicals like Wordsworth and his friends. Poor harvests brought hunger, and in Cornwall and Devon labourers wearing skirts to look like housewives marched through villages crying, 'We cannot starve.'[3] In Bath, in 1796, Samuel Taylor Coleridge preached his first sermon, startling the 'large and enlightened' Unitarian congregation by his bright blue coat and by his text: 'When they shall be hungry they shall fret themselves, and curse their king and their God and look upward' [Isaiah 8:21].[4]

It was at Racedown, in early 1797, that Wordsworth wrote the first version of 'The Ruined Cottage', telling the story of Margaret, sliding into decline as she clings to hope that her soldier husband will return.[5] (See fig. 11 for the Alfoxden notebook which includes the manuscript of 'The Ruined Cottage'.) A year later, after moving to Alfoxden in Somerset to be near Coleridge, where they worked together on the poems that became the *Lyrical Ballads* — and were suspected of being spies — Wordsworth added the frame, in which the Pedlar tells the tale to the poet on a

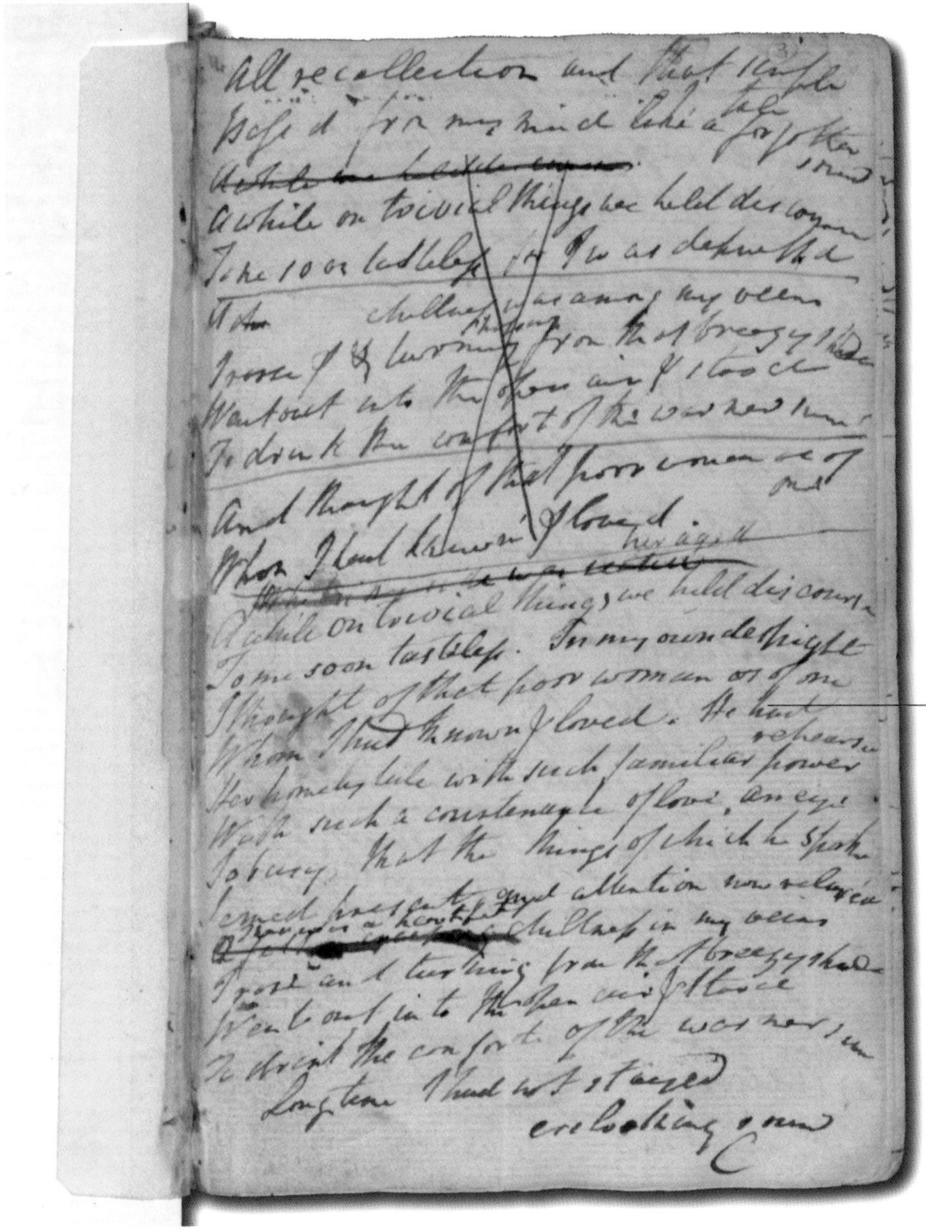

'He had rehearsed / Her homely tale with such familiar power / With such a countenance of love, an eye / So busy, and the things of which he spake / Semed present ...' [266–70]

Figure 11. William Wordsworth (1770–1850), Alfoxden Notebook, lines towards 'The Ruined Cottage', 1798.

hot summer day in the neglected cottage garden. Margaret's husband, we learn, was a weaver, 'an industrious man / Sober and steady' [172–3], but their life was blighted by two terrible harvests and then,

> A worse affliction in the plague of war:
> A happy land was stricken to the heart;
> 'Twas a sad time of sorrow and distress. [188–90]

They struggle on until his illness eats up their savings and he can find no work. Taking the bounty for enlisting, he disappears 'to a distant land' [328]; later their oldest son becomes 'a serving boy / Apprenticed by the parish' [404–5] and the baby dies. As Margaret waits for news, accosting everyone who passes, her cottage and garden decay.

Poverty and war enter this Eden like the serpent:

> ... She is dead,
> And nettles rot and adders sun themselves
> Where we have sat together while she nursed
> Her infant at her bosom. [162–65]

The story of a single woman in a particular place is thus also a general one. At the coming of war, the rich, the Pedlar says,

> Sunk down as in a dream among the poor,
> And of the poor did many cease to be,
> And their place knew them not ... [194–96]

It was true that when the conflict began, stocks lost value and banks stopped loans. 'In Wheelers *Manchester Chronicle* of August 31st,' noted the Oldham weaver William Rowbottom in 1793, 'it apeared that since January last owing to these dismal times no less than 873 Commisions of Bankrupsey had been issued out.'[6] As the years went on, upper-and middle-class families found it hard to pay the ever-rising taxes and the less well-off continued to suffer. 'War is life to the contractor, and death to the landed man', declared the Denbighshire MP Thomas Jones in 1799. 'War is life to the loan-jobber, and death to the peasant ... life to the clothier and death to the labourer.'[7]

Hunger and bread riots had followed the terrible winter of 1798–9, when William and Dorothy froze in their German lodgings. On New Year's Day 1799 Rowbottom noted, 'Roast Beef Pyes and Ale are not to be seen in the poor mans table on the contery it is graced with Misery and Want and a universal lowness of spirits and dejected countinance appear in every one.'[8] As late as mid-May, snowdrifts lay on the fields. There was no hay for the horses, livestock suffered and the price of meat rose. In the textile towns many small masters, unable to find credit, laid off men, and the Lancashire cotton weavers and Yorkshire wool finishers began to unite to petition for regulation of their wages. In response Pitt's government passed the Combination Acts, banning workers' organisations. Like Margaret's husband, many weavers enlisted just to get the bounty, their choice recorded in the Lancashire ballad 'John O'Grinfilt'. As Wordsworth's Pedlar in 'The Ruined Cottage' notes:

> … shoals of artisans
>
> Were from their daily labour turned away
>
> To hang for bread on parish charity [206–8]

Parish relief itself caused problems. Some local towns had workhouses, but when Frederick Eden toured Britain in 1797 he found that in Carlisle, for example, people preferred 'the chance of starving among friends and neighbours in their own village' rather than joining 'idiots and vagrants' in the workhouse.[9] The Poor Law Guardians were fiercely vigilant, and people from elsewhere were often sent back to their original parish: if that parish would not accept them they were doomed to walk the roads. The Guardians also turned down anyone who might make a living, including a poor hatter who called at Dove Cottage in June 1800. He had been ill and his wife was about to give birth, but the parish would not accept him 'because he had implements of trade &c — &c — We gave him 6d' [DWJ 20 June 1801].

Children taken in by the parish were sent to work, like Margaret's son: a 'serving-boy' meant that he was bound for 'a term of servitude', usually seven years. Many were sent to the textile mills springing up in the Pennine valleys and northern towns: leaving Keswick in the dusk in November 1800 Dorothy noted 'Cotton mills lighted up' [DWJ 7 Dec 1801]. When the Birmingham Poor Law Guardians visited their parish apprentices at Robert Peel's Lancashire factories in 1796, they found long hours, homesickness and brutality. Seeing children without shoes or stockings, they were told that 'if they gave them shoes they would run away'.[10] Some manufacturers treated apprentices well, like Samuel Gregg at Quarry Bank and the linen magnate John Marshall, the husband of Dorothy's childhood friend Jane Pollard, but all of them used cheap labour to build their fortunes. More and more women, too, stopped spinning at home and went to the mill, but the domestic industry continued, with women taking over the men's traditional weaving role. As the Wigan magistrate John Singleton noted in May 1799, 'Altho' numbers of our people are gone for soldiers and sailors there is still an increase in Looms for if a man enlists, his Wife turns Weaver (for here the women are weavers as well as the men) and instructs her children in the art of weaving.'[11]

In December 1801, Wordsworth turned again to Margaret's weaver husband and her 'homely tale'. (See fig. 12 for James Gillray's visual depiction of war's destruction of the home.) Two days before Christmas a thaw came, but 'it was a thick black heavy air', wrote Dorothy,

> I baked pies and bread. Mary wrote out the Tales from Chaucer for Coleridge. William workd at The Ruined Cottage & made himself very ill. I went to bed without dinner, he went to the other bed — we both slept & Mary lay on the Rug before the Fire. A broken soldier came to beg in the morning. [DWJ 23 Dec 1801]

Figure 12. James Gillray (1756–1815), *John Bulls Progress*, 1793. © Trustees of the British Museum.

The conjunction of 'The Ruined Cottage' and the soldier on the road is a touching coincidence. At Alfoxden, Wordsworth had also composed 'The Discharged Soldier', which became part of *The Prelude*,[12] with his 'uncouth shape' [IV, 386] in the moonlit lane, propped against a mile-stone, 'Stiff, lank and upright' [IV, 392]:

> … Companionless,
>
> No dog attending, by no staff sustained
>
> He stood; and in his very dress appeared
>
> A desolation, a simplicity
>
> To which the trappings of a gaudy world
>
> Make a strange background. [IV, 398–403]

The soldier explains that he has served in the Tropics, been discharged and is now walking towards his 'native home' [IV, 424], but he speaks of the war with 'a strange half-absence' [IV, 442], as if numb to feeling. With 'His ghostly figure moving at my side' [IV, 433], Wordsworth presents him as kind of double of the people at home, who know about the war only from newspapers and letters, windows ajar on horrors they cannot really understand, and those involved often choose not to speak of. Home, the 'peculiar nook of earth' ['The Ruined Cottage' 132], is the key: for Margaret, who refuses to leave her cottage, for the discharged soldier, and for the poet who leaves him and seeks 'with quiet heart my distant home' [*Prelude* IV, 468]. But what kind of 'home' did wartime life offer?

A labourer takes the soldier in: 'the cottage door was speedily unbarred' [IV, 460]. But labourers and small-holders faced their own problems. Life was hard. As food ran short and the profits from grain and meat rose, keen-eyed men moved in, eyeing farms 'as a merchant would view a pound weight of raisins'.[13] Walking to Rydal in May 1800, Dorothy met her neighbour John Fisher: 'He talked much about the alteration in the times, & observed that in a short time there would be only two ranks of people, the very rich and the very poor, for those who have small estates says he are forced to sell, & all the land goes into one hand' [DWJ 19 (18) May 1800]. Ten years later, in writing which later became his *Guide to the Lakes*, Wordsworth noted that rising costs had made it impossible for many small independent 'statesmen' of the area to survive. Their already mortgaged lands, he wrote, 'fall into the hands of wealthy purchasers, who in like manner unite and consolidate; and, if they wish to become residents, erect new mansions out of the ruins of the ancient cottages, whose little enclosures, with all the wild graces that grew out of them, disappear'.[14]

Even small farmers, like Wordsworth's future brother-in-law Jack Hutchinson, at Sockburn in County Durham, became speculators if they could. In May 1799, he told his cousin John Monkhouse that he was

> going into the Butter Trade this summer & any
>
> of my Customers that you see you may tell them
>
> so — You may tell Mr Wilson that he need not
>
> be afraid of making money of his Hams — he
>
> may rest assured that in a little Time everything
>
> of Provisions will be extravagantly dear …

Butter must be very scarce & I am determined
to speculate in the Article as far as prudence &
Cash will permit.[15]

The 'Bacon business' proved successful at first, but by December 1801 Jack was complaining that pigs were now so scarce that their prices were soaring. 'Nick Nottle the great Bacon & Pork man at Penrith has failed', he wrote, and now local banks were going under. Later in the war, in 1808, Jack's brother Tom and John Monkhouse hunted for months before finding a farm they could afford, at Hindwell in Radnorshire. They won prizes at the newly formed Radnorshire Agricultural Society but still found it hard going. Trying to sell his wool, Tom sought advice on future prices 'to be upon our guard against the cunning wool buyers in this country'.[16] When Napoleon returned from Elba, Tom's wife, Mary, believed the farmers — who had feared peace would lower corn prices — were generally pleased. More than half of them, who 'think of themselves alone and look no further than the present would be most happy to have war again'.[17]

Agricultural 'improvement' affected life across the country. One of its keenest advocates was John Christian Curwen, who founded the Workington Agricultural Society in 1805, based at his model farm at the Schoose, with four districts: Keswick, Wigton, Cockermouth and Egremont. One prizewinner was Thomas King, a Leicester man who moved from Rydal Mount to the Hollens in Grasmere in 1802, and was praised as 'an admirable specimen of the effects of cultivation' (although his ugly barn and 'his Fir larch plantations, that look like a blotch or scar' certainly offended his Wordsworth neighbours).[18] Curwen was also delighted that the rate of enclosure had trebled. In the Lake District stone walls climbed higher and higher up the mountains, reflecting, as he put it to the Society, a 'disposition to carry the plough much nearer heaven than what was dreamed of a few years ago'.[19] But while they suffered less than the Highlanders driven off their land by the clearances, few dispossessed cottagers rejoiced.

It was not all gloom. In the country towns there were assemblies and balls, new theatres and schools were opened, races were held and the markets and fairs stayed busy. John Clare, remembering his childhood in Northamptonshire, wrote that 'the year was crowned with holidays'.[20] There was Christmas, with ivy branches and morris dancers; Valentine's Day, Shrove Tuesday, April Fool's Day and St Mark's Eve, 24 April, when girls baked a 'dumb' cake to eat silently at midnight and walked backwards to see 'the likeness of their sweethearts hurrying after them'.[21] May Day had races and maypoles, the summer brought feasts for haymaking, sheep shearing and rushbearing; the autumn had fairs and harvest home.

As the seasons changed, so the trees greened and browned and budded again. When he revised 'The Ruined Cottage', Wordsworth ended with the Pedlar's injunction to find solace in the natural world — good advice for the growth of a poet's mind, perhaps, but hardly helpful to the likes of Margaret. In 1809–10, when Wordsworth put her story into his draft of *The Excursion* (1814), British trade and manufacturing were hit hard by Napoleon's closure of continental ports and the British 'Orders in Council', banning trade with French-held territories. The textile workers' protests against the new machines, culminating in the Luddite troubles of 1812, overlapped with huge popular meetings clamouring for peace.

When peace came in 1814 it was greeted by nationwide excitement, only to be dashed by Napoleon's return from Elba: once again the recruiting officers were out in the country and the towns. After the final, hard-won victory at Waterloo, Britain emerged as a thrusting industrial nation with a growing empire. But the close of war in 1815 was not the end of the struggle: in the depression that followed, the men marching home, exhausted and scarred, and the working people who cheered them faced a hard and uncertain future.

(Endnotes)

1. A date preceded by 'DWJ' indicates that the quotation will be found by date in *The Grasmere and Alfoxden Journals*, Oxford World's Classics, ed. Pamela Woof (Oxford: Oxford University Press, 2002)

2. *The Letters of William and Dorothy Wordsworth*, ed. E. de Selincourt; *The Early Years, 1787–1805*, rev. Chester L Shaver (Oxford: Oxford University Press, 1967), 162

3. John Bohstedt, *The Politics of Provisions: Food Riots, Moral Economy and Market Transition in England, c.1550–1850* (Farnham: Ashgate Publishing, 2010), 174–7

4. Joseph Cottle, *Early Recollections*, 2 vols. (London: Longman, Rees & Company, 1837), I, 178–9. Cottle dates this 1796, but John Beer plausibly suggested Sept/Oct 1795 in *Coleridge the Visionary* (London: Chatto & Windus,1959), 70

5. 1798 text. Quotations are taken from *The Poems of William Wordsworth, Collected Reading Texts from The Cornell Wordsworth*, ed. Jared Curtis, 3 vols. (Ithaca: Cornell University Press e-books, 2012), I, 270–85. For manuscript revisions made in 1799, 1801–2 and 1809–12, see *The Ruined Cottage and The Pedlar by William Wordsworth*, ed. James Butler (Ithaca, New York: Cornell University Press, 1979)

6. William Rowbottom diary, transcript, Oldham Library

7. William Cobbett, *Parliamentary History*, XXXIV, (London: R.Bagshaw, 1812), 1429–30

8. Rowbottom, 1 Jan 1799

9. C.M.L. Bouch and G.O. Jones, *A Short Economic History of the Lake Counties, 1500–1830* (Manchester: University of Manchester Press, 1961), 304; Frederick Eden, *The State of the Poor*, 3 vols. (London: B.&J. White, 1797), II, 58

10. Minutes of Birmingham Board of Guardians, 28 June 1796; Katrine Honeyman, *Child Workers in England, 1780–1820: Parish Apprentices and the Making of the Early Industrial Labour Force* (Farnham: Ashgate Publishing, 2007), 253

11. Katrina Navickas, *Loyalism and Radicalism in Lancashire 1798–1815* (Oxford: Oxford University Press, 2008), 24; TNA HO 42/41/1, Singleton to King, 27 May 1799

12. 1850 text. Quotations are taken from *The Prelude 1799, 1805, 1850*, ed. Jonathan Wordsworth, M.H. Abrams and Stephen Gill (New York, London: W.W. Norton & Company, 1979)

13. *The Farmer's Magazine*, VII, (Edinburgh: Archibald Constable & Co., Edinburgh, 1806), 121

14. 1835 text. William Wordsworth, *Guide to the Lakes*, ed. E. de Selincourt (Oxford: Oxford University Press, 1977), 91

15. Wordsworth Trust, WLMS H/1/1/3, John Hutchinson to John Monkhouse, 17, 25 May 1799

16. Wordsworth Trust, WLMS H1/5/1/21, note from Tom Hutchinson, on Mary Monkhouse to Thomas Monkhouse, 6 Aug 1809

17. Wordsworth Trust, H1/5/34 Mary Hutchinson (née Monkhouse) to Tom Monkhouse, 20 March 1815

18. *Report of the Workington Agricultural Society* (Workington: E. Bowness, 1807). See Dorothy Wordsworth's letter to Lady Beaumont, 7 Nov 1805. *The Letters of William and Dorothy Wordsworth*, ed. E. de Selincourt; *The Early Years, 1787–1805*, rev. Chester L. Shaver (Oxford: Oxford University Press 1967), 638; see note to DWJ 1 Dec 1800, 195

19. *The Farmer's Magazine*, VIII, (Edinburgh: Archibald Constable & Co., 1807), 243

20. *John Clare by Himself*, ed. Eric Robinson and David Powell (Manchester: Carcanet Press, 1996), 35

21. John Clare, in *William Hone's Every Day Book*, 1825, in John Wardroper, ed., *The World of William Hone* (London: Shelfmark, 1997), 113–14

Anticipation. October, 1803

William Wordsworth

Shout, for a mighty Victory is won!

On British ground the Invaders are laid low;

The breath of Heaven has drifted them like snow,

And left them lying in the silent sun,

Never to rise again! — the work is done.

Come forth, ye Old Men, now in peaceful show

And greet your Sons! drums beat, and trumpets blow!

Make merry, Wives! ye little Children stun

Your Grandame's ears with pleasure of your noise!

Clap, Infants, clap your hands! Divine must be

That triumph, when the very worst, the pain,

And even the prospect of our Brethren slain,

Hath something in it which the heart enjoys: —

In glory will they sleep and endless sanctity.

WORDSWORTH & THE SHEPHERDS AGAINST NAPOLEON

RICHARD MATLAK

❦

I T   IS   DIFFICULT to imagine that residents of the sequestered Lake District could be aroused to arms by a war on the Continent. Yet in 1803, when Napoleon made clear his intention to invade the United Kingdom, he aroused the entire population with the Great Terror. To adapt Wordsworth's comment about the ubiquity of spring,[1] the alarm of invasion also left 'no corner of the land untouched'. London newspapers reported in June 1803 that the French army in the port of Boulogne, the nursery of the invasion, had reached a strength of 80,000. *The London Gazette* concluded gloomily 'there is very little doubt' that the forces and the gathering vessels were 'destined for the meditated attack on this country'. By October 1803, the French Minister of Marine reported that the size of the flotilla had grown to 1367 vessels and that the forces massing at Boulogne were 150,000 strong. Napoleon's audacious goal was transparent: 'it is necessary for us to be masters of the sea for six hours only, and England will have ceased to exist'.[2]

Fantasies of invasion became the stuff of nightmares. Indeed, it was the advice of Prime Minister William Pitt to 'Expect the French every dark night.'[3] Such fantasies went back at least as far as the earlier French invasion threat of 1798, as is illustrated by James Gillray's cartoon *The Storm rising; — or — the Republican Flotilla in danger* (see fig. 13) which depicts a vast Gallic army aboard an extraordinary landing craft being pulled across the English Channel by a number of opposition politicians, including Charles James Fox.

As one response to the credible threat of invasion, the English built Martello towers in Ireland, Scotland and along the southeast coast of England to counter the vessels of invading forces: 27 in Kent; 42 in East Sussex; 3 in Scotland; 50 in Ireland; 1 in Wales; and 1 in the Channel Islands. The towers contained floors for housing soldiers, storing ammunition and emplacing armaments.

The most critical defensive measure was to raise a large and flexible home force to repel an invasion that might well have multiple landing sites. In a great display of 'national defence patriotism',[4] an army of volunteers from peers to peasants over 350,000 strong signed on to defend the kingdom. The Crown published a poster in 1806 to commemorate 'the Great and United Spirit of the British People, Armed for the Support of their Ancient Glory and Independence Against the Unprincipled Ambition of the French Government' (see fig. 14):[5] King George leading from the

The Storm rising; — or — the Republican FLOTILLA in danger.

Figure 13. James Gillray (1756–1815), *The Storm rising; — or — the Republican Flotilla in danger*, 1798. © Trustees of the British Museum.

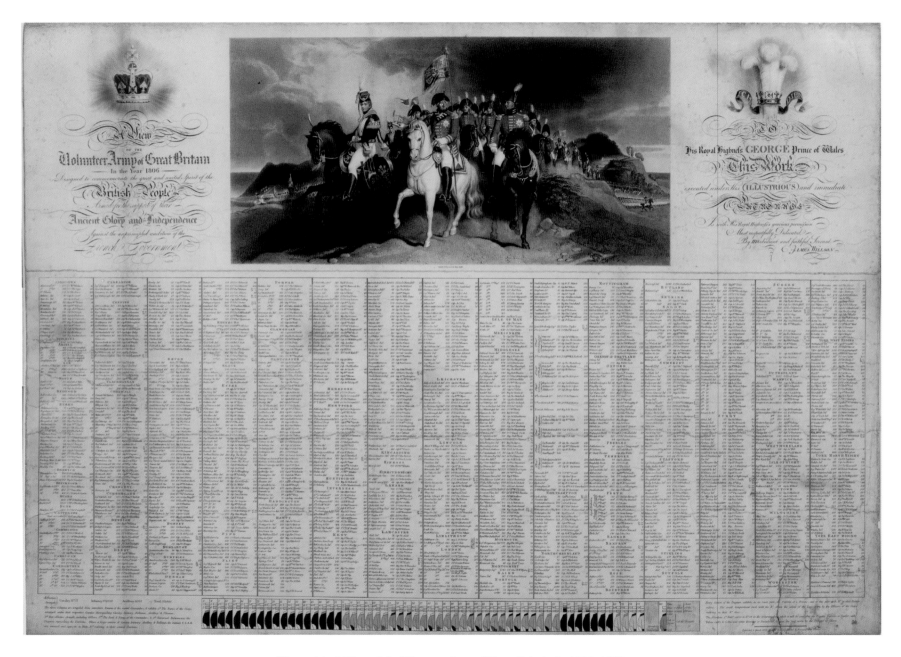

Figure 14. *A View of the Volunteer Army of Great Britain in 1806–1807*,
reproduced with kind permission of Cumbria Archive Centre, Kendal.

front on his white stallion, flanked by senior officers, with volunteer cavalry behind, and infantrymen stretching into infinity on both sides of an island provide a dramatic visual of a united mass to combat Napoleon. Hero-worship aside, the alphabetical listing of counties and their volunteer units below the engraving certainly gave the British nation the security it required. Included in the rolls are the counties of Westmorland and Cumberland, the homeland of the shepherds and the poets of the Lake District, to which we will now turn (see fig. 15).

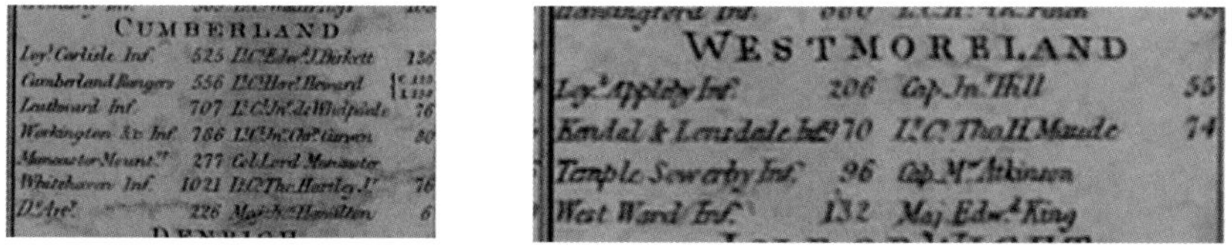

Figure 15. *A View of the Volunteer Army of Great Britain in 1806–1807* (detail), reproduced with kind permission of Cumbria Archive Centre, Kendal.

William Viscount Lowther was Lord-Lieutenant of the counties which are today's Cumbria. Per the Militia Act of 1802 and the oath Lowther took at the Court of St James in 1802, he was the commander of the militia and thus responsible for homeland defence in the area of his lieutenancy. In July 1803, Lord-Lieutenant Lowther began receiving directives from the War Office in London to recruit for the Army of the Reserve and to begin basic training within the month. Additionally, Lowther was directed to 'resort to the Zeal and Public Spirit of the Inhabitants of the count[ies] under [his] charge' to lend their private weapons and for him to distribute

them so that there would be 25 firelocks for every 100 drilling men.[6] The remainder of the men would carry pikes (spear-like weapons about 12 feet in length). If men happened to be in logistical units called Pioneers, they might carry their own shovels.

One Colonel Dirom from the regular forces explained the mission and tactics of these 'irregular forces' in the *Cumberland Pacquet*, a weekly regional newspaper: 'from the first moment of a landing being made the great object of the irregular troops must be to harass, alarm, and fatigue an enemy … without ever engaging in serious action or hazarding themselves …'. Pioneer units of colliers and miners could 'carry entrenching and other tools flung over their shoulders'. They could use their shovels to 'encompass the invading army with a ditch and rampart which it would be difficult, perhaps impossible, for them to pass' [19 July 1803]. Training guidance was also published in the *Pacquet*. It included handling the pike in a military manner, modelled after a traditional 'manual of arms' for a rifle — 'shoulder pike', 'charge pike', 'receive the charge', 'ground pike', etc. [25 Oct 1803]. (A manual of arms for the shovel was never published. See fig. 16 for a contemporary representation of volunteers training.)[7]

Carrying pikes and shovels into battle rather than firearms certainly sounds like a tough sell for recruiting young men; yet, despite inglorious arms, the shepherds, miners, farmers, small tradesmen, gentlemen from prominent families and miscellaneous others signed on. In his accounting to Parliament in December 1803, Lord-Lieutenant Lowther reported raising eight volunteer units in Cumberland, with a total of 3736 men, and four units in Westmorland, with 1420 men, for a grand total of 5156 men.[8] His quota was 5146 men, so he exceeded his quota by 10!

Figure 16. George Cruikshank (1792–1878), *Symptoms of Drilling*, date unknown.

Indeed, the rush to volunteer one's services and to pledge money was contagious. The *Cumberland Pacquet* reports that in August 1803, 'when a book was opened [at Kendal's Town Hall] for enrolling the names of such as chose to come forward as volunteers, … 426 entered their names, and 1000 pounds sterling was immediately subscribed, and the number of volunteers is now increased to nearly 700'. Linda Colley offers stunning documentary evidence of the patriotic spirit in this area 19,322 people from Cumberland and Westmorland signed the public declaration: 'We abhor monarchical tyranny. We still more abhor republican tyranny … Whilst we have life we will not submit to a tyrannical government under any denomination.'[9]

At Grasmere, Wordsworth bragged to his patron Sir George Beaumont that 'we have turned out almost to a man'.[10] In 1801, there were approximately 270 residents in 62 families in Grasmere.[11] How many active volunteers could there have been? Wordsworth's *The Excursion* (1814) provides an historical window into the volunteer movement in Grasmere and the ten young men who regularly marched to Ambleside for military training. Wordsworth himself drilled for a time with the unit, and even got fitted with a red coat, but finally let his patriotic 'Sonnets Dedicated to Liberty', published in *Poems, in Two Volumes* (1807), stand as his contribution to the campaign against Napoleon.

The acknowledged leader of the young men of Grasmere was 'young George Dawson, the first young Man in the vale', as Dorothy wrote.[12] In *The Excursion*, Dawson becomes the character Oswald, whose story is told by the Pastor as he reviews the lives of the unmarked graves in his Grasmere churchyard for the Wanderer, the Solitary and the Poet. It may be that Wordsworth chose Oswald as Dawson's name to suggest a heroic lineage with St Oswald, the warrior king of seventh-century Northumbria and the namesake of Grasmere Church.[13]

For, we are told, the young man was god-like, 'As old Bards / Tell in their idle songs of wandering Gods, / Pan or Apollo, veiled in human form' [VII, 751–3].[14] The sight of him

> … kindled pleasure in all hearts
> By his ingenuous beauty, by the gleam
> Of his fair eyes, by his capacious brow,
> By all the graces with which nature's hand
> Had bounteously arrayed him. [VII, 747–51]

Besides his beauty, Oswald was a natural athlete, a charismatic leader and a 'gallant Teacher' who, with a map spread on the grass, would locate for his peers the territories where battles now 'fiercely raged', such as 'those fatal Fields / On which the Sons of mighty Germany / Were taught a base submission' at Austerlitz[15] [VII, 819–22].

Oswald seemed made for this historical moment when 'in remotest vales was heard — to Arms!' [VII, 784]. His fellow volunteers changed their 'Shepherd's grey to martial scarlet … And graced with shining weapons' (their pikes) followed Oswald 'From their shy solitude, to face the world, / With a gay confidence and seemly pride; / Measuring the soil beneath their happy feet' [VII, 786–98 *passim*] in disciplined march. Obviously, the teenagers were excited by the serious play of soldiering and proud to have Oswald as their leader. Everyone understood, as the Pastor concludes,

'In him the spirit of a Hero walked / Our unpretending valley' [VII, 762–3].

Sadly, Oswald's end is anti-climactic. Fatigued from running with the hounds in a deer hunt, he catches a fever from washing the family sheep in a 'chilling flood' [VII, 890]. After twelve convulsive days, 'nature rested from her work in death' [VII, 895]. His bereaved comrades provide a military funeral. The Pastor recalls the startling volleys of rifles firing three rounds each as Oswald's coffin was lowered into the ground: 'distant mountains echoed with a sound / Of lamentation, never heard before!' [VII, 911–12].

Wordsworth attended Dawson's/Oswald's funeral.[16] It is unsurprising, then, that the Pastor's final words express the sentiments of Wordsworth's invasion sonnets of October 1803. In 'These times touch money'd Worldlings with dismay', the saviours of England will be those 'tens of thousands, … /sound, healthy children of the god of heaven', who remain fearless and 'cheerful as the rising sun in may', while 'money'd worldlings' find that their riches 'are akin / To fear, to change, to cowardice, and death!' George Dawson, the natural-born hero of the common man, stands at the front of those 'healthy children of the god of heaven' as a promise before the Pastor's 'swimming eyes' that 'England, the ancient and the free' would remain 'Unconquerably virtuous and secure' [VII, 876–8].

Nelson's defeat of the combined French and Spanish navies at Trafalgar brought the Great Terror to an end. Had there been an invasion, Wordsworth was certain that the likes of Dawson, leading the shepherds and the common man of England, would prevail when the stakes were 'Victory or Death!'[17]

(Endnotes)

1. *William Wordsworth: The Prelude 1799, 1805, 1850*, ed. Jonathan Wordsworth, M.H. Abrams and Stephen Gill (New York: Norton, 1979), VI, 370

2. Quoted in Frank McLynn, *Invasion: From the Armada to Hitler 1588–1945* (London: Routledge & Kegan Paul, 1987), 107

3. Letter of 3 Oct 1803 from Tom Wedgwood to his brother Josiah. Printed in Richard Buckley Litchfield, *Tom Wedgwood: the First Photographer* (London: Duckworth, 1903), 153

4. The phrase is used by J.E. Cookson in *The British Armed Nation 1793–1815* (Oxford: Clarendon Press, 1997), 7

5. 'A View of the Volunteer Army of Great Britain in 1806–1807'. National Archives. Kendal Archive Centre, in a collection called 'Cumberland and other publications', Ref: WDX 991

6. Lonsdale Papers, National Archives, Carlisle, England

7. *Cumberland Pacquet*, Carlisle City Library, Carlisle, England

8. Lonsdale Papers

9. Linda Colley, *Britons: Forging the Nation 1707–1837* (New Haven: Yale UP, 1992), 312

10. *The Letters of William and Dorothy Wordsworth*, ed. Ernest de Selincourt; *The Early Years, 1787–1805*, rev. Chester L. Shaver (Oxford: Clarendon Press, 1967), 409

11. 'Grasmere Parish History'

12. *Letters of William and Dorothy Wordsworth*, ed. Ernest de Selincourt; *II. The Middle Years, Part I. 1806–1811*, rev. Mary Moorman, (Oxford: Clarendon Press, 1969), 158

13. This is a suggestion made by Kenneth R. Johnston in *Wordsworth and 'The Recluse'* (New Haven: Yale UP, 1984), 310

14. *The Excursion by William Wordsworth*, ed. Sally Bushell, James A. Butler and Michael C. Jaye, (Ithaca: Cornell University Press, 2007)

15. Wordsworth makes an historical error here as the Battle of Austerlitz occurred in December 1805, which is after Nelson's victory at Trafalgar in October 1805, which ended the threat of invasion. In fact, Napoleon's Army of England left Boulogne to fight at Austerlitz.

16. *The Excursion by William Wordsworth*, ed. Sally Bushell, James A. Butler and Michael C. Jaye, (Ithaca: Cornell University Press, 2007), note to lines 720–838, 415

17. 'To the Men of Kent', line 14 and the sonnet 'Anticipation', where the poet imagines 'the Invaders … laid low … like snow, … lying in the silent sun, / Never to rise again!' [2–5]

... the tidings of Lord Nelson's Fate reached us at Patterdale. We were at Breakfast when Mr Luff's Maid-servant opened the door, and, shewing only her head, with an uncouth stare and a grin of pleasure told us that there had been a great victory, and Lord Nelson was shot. It was a blow. I was not collected enough to doubt, and burst into tears; but William would not believe all at once, and forced me to suspend my grief till he had made further inquiries. At the Inn we were told that there were 'great rejoicings at Penrith — all the Bells ringing'. 'Then, I exclaimed, he cannot be dead!' but we soon heard enough to leave us without a doubt, and bitterly did we lament for him and our Country.

Dorothy Wordsworth to Lady Beaumont, 29 Nov 1805

WORDSWORTH'S JAUNT WITH THE SPIRIT OF NELSON,

FROM RYDAL THROUGH GRASMERE TO KESWICK

PAUL F BETZ

BEFORE THERE COULD be Waterloo, there had to be Nelson. His decisive naval encounters with Napoleon's fleets at the Battle of the Nile and at Trafalgar ended the Emperor's options at sea and began the slide toward 1814 and 1815.

A great number of poems were published during this period to commemorate Nelson's major battles and his heroic death. Among these are: Edward Dupre, *On the Victory Obtained by Rear-Admiral Lord Nelson, of the Nile, Over the French Fleet, On the First Day of August, 1798. A Poem.* (published in Jersey), 1798; William Thomas Fitzgerald, *Miscellaneous Poems*, 1801 (includes 'Nelson's Triumph, or the Battle of the Nile'); also by Fitzgerald, *Nelson's Tomb, A Poem. To Which is Added, An Address to England on Her Nelson's Death*, 1805; John Gordon, *Poems* (includes verse on Nelson's death), 1807; Thos. L. Morris, *The Daneid, An Epic Poem, in Four Books, Written on board his Majesty's ship La Desiree* (published c.1803 in Newcastle by a self-described 'rude unletter'd seaman'); [A Naval Officer], *The Cruise: A Poetical Sketch, In Eight Cantos* (this epic poem concludes with the news of Nelson's death in battle), 1808; and John Thelwall, *The Trident of Albion, &c. With an Address To the Shade of Nelson* (privately printed in Liverpool), 1805. Much could be added, and then there is relevant prose (Southey wrote *Life of Horatio Lord Viscount Nelson* (abridged version

1822). Wordsworth's *Benjamin the Waggoner*[1] can be seen, among other things, as the poet's tribute to the fallen hero. (See fig. 17 for a visual tribute to Nelson.)

Of *Benjamin* it may be said, as the Sailor says of his scale model of Nelson's *Vanguard*, '[y]ou'll find you've much in little here!' [394]. In the guise of simplicity, this mock-heroic poem is complex in ways that can barely be touched on in this chapter. The poem was first drafted by Wordsworth in January 1806, when Nelson's victory in 1798 at the Battle of the Nile, although over seven years in the past, was still vivid in the minds of all. It is relevant that both Nelson (at Trafalgar) and John Wordsworth, the poet's brother had lost their lives at sea in 1805. Not one of the poet's better-known works today, *Benjamin* was a great favourite of his and of his family and friends. Charles Lamb praises especially its 'spirit of beautiful tolerance'. Its form draws some appealing, comic qualities from Robert Burns. It is a verse precursor to a slice of Wordsworth's later prose *Guide to the Lakes*, as the waggon slowly moves from Rydal, past Dove Cottage in Grasmere, past the Swan inn, over steep Dunmail Raise, and, after a pause at the village merry-night celebration at the Cherry Tree inn in Wythburn (see fig. 18), past the Rock of Names on Thirlmere and at last to Keswick. In the 1819 version, unaccompanied by the motley band, Wordsworth's 'sage Muse'

Figure 17. Unknown artist and engraver, *Britannia bringing her Dead Hero to Britannia's shore*, 1806.

even takes a side excursion through St John's Vale. The lovable but feckless Benjamin is the anti-hero: only he can persuade his horses to pull the very large waggon over the somewhat primitive, and at times very steep, road.

Crucial to the action is an encounter with a gruff Sailor, his wife and babe, at Dunmail Raise in the midst of a terrific storm. Kind Benjamin lets the woman and her babe take cover in his waggon; in gratitude, the Sailor promises to buy him a drink at the Cherry Tree.[2] (Soon, Nelson's spectre will appear in vivid, symbolic form, conjured up by the Sailor.) Thus the story continues:

> A steaming Bowl — a blazing fire —
> What greater good can heart desire?
> …
> The CHERRY TREE shows proof of this;
> For soon, of all the happy there,
> Our Travellers are the happiest pair.
> All care with Benjamin is gone —
> A Cæsar past the Rubicon!
> He thinks not of his long, long strife; —
> The Sailor, Man by nature gay,
> Hath no resolves to throw away;
> And he hath now forgot his Wife,
> …
> While thus our jocund Travellers fare,
> Up springs the Sailor from his chair —

> Limps (for I might have told before
> That he was lame) across the floor —
> Is gone — returns — and with a prize;
> With what? — a Ship of lusty size;
> A gallant stately Man of War,
> Fix'd on a smoothly-sliding car.
> Surprise to all, but most surprise
> To Benjamin, who rubs his eyes,
> Not knowing that he had befriended
> A Man so gloriously attended!
>
> 'This,' cries the Sailor, 'a third-rate is —
> Stand back and you shall see her gratis!
> This was the Flag Ship at the Nile,
> The Vanguard — you may smirk and smile,
> But, pretty maid, if you look near,
> You'll find you've much in little here!
> A nobler Ship did never swim.
> And you shall see her in full trim;
> I'll set, my Friends, to do you honour,
> Set every inch of sail upon her.'
> So said, so done; and masts, sails, yards,
> He names them all; and interlards
> His speech with uncouth terms of art,

Figure 18. Drawing of The Cherry Tree Inn, Wythburn, possibly by Dora Wordsworth (1804–1847). © Professor Paul F Betz.

Accomplish'd in the Showman's part;

And then, as from a sudden check,

Cries out — ''Tis there, the Quarter-deck

On which brave Admiral Nelson stood —

A sight that would have rous'd your blood!

One eye he had, which, bright as ten,

Burnt like a fire among his men;

Let this be Land, and that be Sea,

Here lay the French — and *thus* came we!' [345–410]

This is much closer than any of the good country people at the merry night are likely to come to Admiral Nelson himself, even although here only through a spectre summoned by this accomplished rustic showman. The lame Sailor, as elsewhere Coleridge's Ancient Mariner and Keats' Belle Dame, holds them in thrall.

    Hush'd was by this the fiddle's sound,

The Dancers all were gathered round,

And such the stillness of the house

You might have heard a nibbling mouse;

While, borrowing helps where'er he may,

The Sailor through the story runs

Of Ships to Ships and guns to guns;

And does his utmost to display

The dismal conflict, and the might

And terror of that wondrous night!

'A Bowl, a Bowl of double measure,'

Cries Benjamin, 'A draught of length,

To Nelson, England's pride and treasure,

Her bulwark and her tower of strength!' [411–24]

Good Benjamin's downfall is now well under way. We have seen him gaze longingly at Dove Cottage (a former inn) and the Swan inn before being tempted into the Cherry Tree by the somewhat Mephisthophelean Sailor. Yet he is on notice from his Master that if he is delayed once more by alcoholic indulgence – there is clearly a history of such incidents — his job will be forfeit. His team of horses, creatures of nature who wish to protect him, have halted at the inn only 'reluctantly'. Soon their accompanying mastiff, another natural creature with similar sympathies, makes a further effort to thwart Benjamin's self-destruction:

When Benjamin had seized the bowl,

The Mastiff, from beneath the wagon,

Where he lay, watchful as a dragon,

Rattled his chain — 'twas all in vain,

For Benjamin, triumphant soul!

He heard the monitory growl;

Heard — and in opposition quaff'd

A deep, determined, desperate draught!

Nor did the battered tar forget,

Or flinch from what he deem'd his debt;
Then like a hero, crown'd with laurel,
Back to her place the ship he led;
Wheel'd her back in full apparel;
And so, flag flying at mast-head,
Re-yoked her to the Ass: — anon,
Cries Benjamin, 'We must be gone.'
Thus, after two hours' hearty stay,
Again behold them on their way! [425–42]

Finally this motley company — waggoner, drunken and feckless Benjamin, the lame Sailor and his wife, babe and ass, the horses and mastiff, and at last

The VANGUARD, following close behind,
Sails spread, as if to catch the wind! [509–10]

set off for Keswick, where on the outskirts the impatient Master waits to decree the inevitable fate

Which robbed us of good Benjamin; —
And of his stately Charge, which none
Could keep alive when He was gone! [845–7]

What did Wordsworth think of Nelson? Few might suppose this question needed asking, even though the implied enthusiasm for the Admiral comes from the Sailor showman and his audience in the Cherry Tree, rather than from Wordsworth directly. There has been no obvious reason to suppose that the poet is not in full sympathy with his fictional audience. However, during a recent Wordsworth Summer Conference in Rydal, Professor John Williams of the University of Greenwich presented a paper with a challenging original view: 'Wordsworth's Alternative Epic, or: Lord Nelson's Part in the Decline and Fall of Honest Benjamin the Waggoner'. Here, the war with Napoleon is seen as, in part, 'Nelson's war … being waged … out of an unhealthy lust for power …'. One might question whether anyone other than an academic, even though a thoughtful and ingenious one, would reach a conclusion apparently so far from the evident direction of the poem. Williams often expresses his views with emphatic certainty: 'Wordsworth makes a specific and unambiguous connection between the evil represented by the sailor, and the spirit in which the war with France was then being conducted; and this in turn is unambiguously associated with Nelson'. This is a mock-heroic poem and, for example, while the Sailor may be a mock-Mephistopheles, he is surely not the very devil. Still, Williams compels us to re-examine our assumptions; and his observations concerning the deaths of Nelson and Wordsworth's brother John, and how these may relate to Wordsworth's poem 'Character of the Happy Warrior', are only a few of the points of interest.

The narrative voice of *Benjamin* is clearly Wordsworth's. But this is a Wordsworth who treats himself humorously. He is the 'simple water-drinking Bard', who with the other 'honest folk within' the much-changed Dove Cottage first hears the waggon 'on the stir! … Along the banks of Rydal Mere'. They soon hear Benjamin leading his team and waggon past 'the DOVE and OLIVE-BOUGH', which no longer offers 'a greeting of good ale / To all who entered Grasmere Vale', but instead

... a Poet harbours now, —

A simple water-drinking Bard;

Why need our Hero then (though frail

His best resolves) be on his guard? —

He marches by secure and bold, —

Yet, while he thinks on times of old,

It seems that all looks wond'rous cold:

He shrugs his shoulders — shakes his head —

And, for the honest folk within,

It is a doubt with Benjamin

Whether they be alive or dead! [59–69]

As the poems winds towards its end, Wordsworth addresses the reader directly, and the impact of the loss of Benjamin and his imposing waggon to Grasmere is central:

Forgive me, then; for I had been

On friendly terms with this Machine:

In him, while he was wont to trace

Our roads, through many a long year's space,

A living Almanack had we;

We had speaking Diary,

That, in this uneventful place

Gave to the days a mark and name

By which we knew them when they came. [794–802]

The Bard and 'all about me here' have seen the waggon pass in all seasons, notably through

... a summer's morning;

While Grasmere smooth'd her liquid plain

The moving image to detain ... [809–11]

Benjamin is gone, but his memory lingers in the thoughts of the simple Bard of Dove Cottage and his circle of friends and family in Grasmere; they can still see in the mind's eye the vanished waggoner and his majestic waggon mirrored in the still water of the lake.

(Endnotes)

1. Finally published in revised form in 1819 as *The Waggoner*, the version quoted here. For an extended examination of this poem, with detailed texts, see The Cornell Wordsworth series *Benjamin the Waggoner*, ed. Paul F. Betz, (Ithaca, New York: Cornell University Press, 1981; rev. 1988)
I thank Carol Anne Rosen for assistance with this chapter.

2. Thus written in 1805. In the 1819 text, it is less clear who will pay.

From Ode. The Morning of the Day Appointed for a General
Thanksgiving. January 18, 1816
William Wordsworth

    Nor will the God of peace and love
    Such martial service disapprove. ...

For Thou art angry with thine enemies!
    For these, and for our errors,
    And sins that point their terrors,
We bow our heads before Thee, and we laud
And magnify thy name, Almighty God!
    But thy most dreaded instrument,
    In working out a pure intent,
    Is Man — arrayed for mutual slaughter, —
    Yea, Carnage is thy daughter! [260–282]

WORDSWORTH, WAR & CHURCH-GOING

PHILIP SHAW

ON FRIDAY 19 April 1793, two months after Britain's entry into the war against Revolutionary France, devout church-goers, in observance of a decree issued by King George III for a day of fasting and national 'humiliation', uttered prayers 'for the pardon of our sins' and for God's 'Blessing and Assistance on THE ARMS OF HIS MAJESTY, by Sea and Land'.[1] Wordsworth emerges in this period as a complex, contradictory and shadowy figure: at the beginning of the year he had published two volumes of verse with the liberal publisher Joseph Johnson and had come dangerously close to outing himself as the 'Republican' author of an incendiary attack on the Anglican clergyman and former revolutionary sympathiser Richard Watson, the Bishop of Llandaff.[2] At the same time, in need of funds to support the French mother of his illegitimate child, Wordsworth had petitioned his uncle William Cookson for a curacy in Harwich, Essex, a petition that his uncle declined on account of his nephew's near-treasonable infatuation with republican politics. It was this rejection that most likely prompted the composition of Wordsworth's attack on Watson.

That the poet would have joined in with the prayers for victory in the spring of 1793 seems unlikely, yet the counter-factual image of a young man recently installed in a provincial parish, imploring divine aid in 'our warfare against an Enemy to all Christian Kings, Princes and States', is perhaps not so difficult to imagine.[3] Certainly the role of parish priest was easy enough for Wordsworth's fellow traveller in France, and possible fellow republican, Robert Jones, to adopt. When, in the early autumn, Wordsworth visited Jones in Plas-yn-Llan, Wales, he would have heard his friend intoning state-sanctioned prayers for the triumph of legitimacy over atheism and republicanism.[4] How the radical author of *A Letter to the Bishop of Llandaff* might have responded to such prayers, delivered in the region presided over by the detested subject of this letter, is recorded in Book X of *The Prelude*:[5]

> It was a grief —
> Grief call it not, 'twas any thing but that —
> A conflict of sensations without name,
> Of which he only who may love the sight
> Of a village steeple as I do can judge,

When in the congregation, bending all

To their great Father, prayers were offered up

Or praises for our country's victories,

And, 'mid the simple worshippers perchance

I only, like an uninvited guest

Whom no one owned, sate silent — shall I add,

Fed on the day of vengeance yet to come! [X, 263–74]

The shift in perspective, from the ardent Jacobin who, in the wake of the Duke of York's defeat at the Battle of Hondschoote on 6 September, 'Exulted in the triumph of my soul / When Englishmen by thousands were o'erthrown' [260–61] to the shamed recollection (ten years later) of one who 'sate silent' when 'prayers were offered up' for 'victories' [270–73], a recollection narrated from the point of view of one brought back into communion with the Church [266–7], drives home the point that 'conflict' [265] for Wordsworth, then as now, was fought as much within as without. Like that other 'uninvited guest', the Ancient Mariner, who in Coleridge's poem haunts the margins of a ceremony in which individuals pledge allegiance to each other and to God, the poet is presented here as a man at odds with himself and with the world. Perhaps too, as the literary critic Kenneth Johnston has suggested, there is a memory here of that missed and, for national, religious and political reasons, impossible ceremony — the wedding service that would have united the English Protestant radical, William Wordsworth, with the French Catholic royalist, Annette Vallon (see fig. 19 for Annette's portrait). When in February 1793, as *The Prelude*

Figure 19. Unknown artist, portrait of Annette Vallon.

records, Britain joined in the war against France the 'ravage of this most unnatural strife' [X, 249] was thus experienced by Wordsworth as 'a civil war dividing his own family'.[6]

In light of the connection established between the outbreak of war and the observance, or his own lack of observance, of prayers in 1793 it seems fitting that Wordsworth should choose to commemorate the end of war in 1815 with a poem intended for a day of national thanksgiving. Wordsworth, by now a confirmed supporter of the Anglican establishment, may well have attended St Oswald's Church in Grasmere on 2 July 1815, joining in with prayers for the 'Glorious Victory obtained over the *French* on Sunday the Eighteen of June, at Waterloo'. Six months later, on Thursday 18 January 1816, the day set aside for a general national thanksgiving, the former republican would most likely have uttered 'Amen' in response to calls for the 're-establishment … of legitimate authority and moral order among the distracted nations of Europe'.[7] Wordsworth, no longer a silent witness to collective expressions of triumph, appears on the basis of this evidence and on the sentiments of joy expressed in his 'Thanksgiving Ode' and its accompanying shorter poems to be ardent and assured in his enthusiasm for the defeat of imperial France. (See fig. 20 for an image of the defeated French Emperor, sent to Wordsworth by Heugh Parry in the summer of 1815.)

The choice of form for the 'Thanksgiving Ode', a version of the ancient Greek *epithalamion*, an extended lyric in praise of a bride and groom to be sung at the door of the wedding chamber, appears, at first glance, to be an unusual choice for a poem written in celebration of a national victory. The literary scholar Eric C. Walker has

Figure 20. Drawing of Napoleon in a letter from Heugh Parry to William Wordsworth, 29 July 1815.

speculated that Wordsworth, in adopting this form, may well have wished to silently acknowledge the recent wedding of his French daughter, Caroline Wordsworth-Vallon.[8] Born in December 1792, on the cusp of hostilities between Britain and France, Caroline could well have figured in the poet's mind as an emblem of domestic discord, one that extended to the division between Britain and France. Despite the fact that Wordsworth failed to attend his daughter's wedding (echoes here of the failed act of union with Annette) the marriage that took place on 28 February 1816 might have appeared as symbolic confirmation that the traumatic breaks and missed encounters of 1792–3 had at last been healed.

The poem itself, however, does not lend itself so easily to such a reading; indeed, for most readers the poem is remembered not so much as a celebration of union than as an unsettling affirmation of 'Carnage' as the 'daughter' of God [282].[9] William Hazlitt, writing a review of a performance of Shakespeare's *Coriolanus* published in December 1816 in *The Examiner*, just ten months after the appearance of Wordsworth's poem, seized upon the grammatically ambiguous closing pronouncement 'Yea, Carnage is thy daughter' as evidence of how 'the language of poetry naturally falls in with the language of power'.[10] The baton was then taken up by Shelley in his savage parody of Wordsworth, 'Peter Bell the Third' (1819):[11]

> Then Peter wrote odes to the Devil; —
> In one of which he meekly said: —
> 'May Carnage and Slaughter,
> They niece and thy daughter,

> May Rapine and Famine,
> Thy gorge ever cramming,
> Glut thee with living and dead!' [634–40]

A few years later Lord Byron, less shocked and perhaps less surprised by Wordsworth's political apostasy, recalled the offending lines in a passage on the Battle of Waterloo in *Don Juan*:[12]

> 'Carnage' (so Wordsworth tells you) 'is God's daughter:'
> If *he* speak truth, she is Christ's sister, and
> Just now behaved as in the Holy Land. [Canto VIII, Stanza IX]

In a note to the passage Byron comments: 'this is perhaps as pretty a pedigree for Murder as ever was found out by Garter King at Arms. — What would have been said, had any free-spoken people discovered such a lineage?'[13] Defending Byron's critique of Wordsworth's lines in an essay published in *Fiction, Fair and Foul* (1880), John Ruskin would conclude that 'the death of the innocent in battle carnage' is not 'His "instrument for working out a pure intent," as Mr. Wordsworth puts it; but Man's instrument for working out an impure one'.[14]

That Wordsworth was himself troubled by 'Carnage is thy daughter' is implied by the alteration of the lines in the 1845 *Poems* to the less contentious

But Man is Thy most awful instrument,

In working out a pure intent;

Thou cloth'st the wicked in their dazzling mail,

And for thy righteous purpose they prevail. [106–9][15]

The original lines have since been defended on the grounds that they force readers 'to inspect the total implications of their rejoicing', forcing them to consider the human costs of victory.[16] It should also be born in mind that in expressing such opinion Wordsworth was not out of line with official church doctrine. In 1794 the Reverend Samuel Humfrays, referring his congregation to Isaiah 34:6 ('The sword of the LORD is filled with blood'), declared 'This then is the true Faith, that we believe and confess, that War with all its train of Miseries, Rapine, Conflagration, and Carnage is the *Act of God*'.[17]

I would suggest that what the poet had in mind in 1816 could be related in other ways to his experience of the effects of war in the 1790s. In Book X of *The Prelude*, Wordsworth follows the account of his uneasy responses to Anglican victory prayers with an extended description of how, in France, 'Domestic carnage now filled all the year' [329]. He then goes on to describe the effects of the Terror in terms that seem to have, as Kenneth Johnston suggests, a deep, personal resonance: like William and Annette, in line 331 the 'maiden' is separated 'from the bosom of her love' and, in the following line, in anticipation of the possible fate of Annette and Caroline, 'the mother' is taken 'from the cradle of her babe'.[18] In lines 327–45 the image of the motherless (and fatherless?) child is sustained in the description of

the revolutionaries as children of 'heinous appetites', toying with a 'windmill', which 'at arm's length', they 'front against the blast … / To make it whirl the faster'. Since Wordsworth was not present for the birth of his child, one wonders to what extent the poem's earlier allusions to the 'solid birth-right' of a republic 'Redeem'd according to example given / By ancient Lawgivers' [186–8] is informed by feelings of guilt and concern for ensuring the legitimacy of his progeny. Might illegitimacy, in both the familial and the political senses of the word, be responsible for conflict at all levels of society?

By way of an answer to this question Wordsworth's 'Thanksgiving Ode' contends the illegitimate child is, nevertheless, a daughter of God; viewed from a providential perspective the devastation she wreaks upon the world may be understood as the 'working out' of 'a pure intent'. When, in 1820, some years after peace was concluded with France, the Wordsworths at last made their journey to France, reuniting father and child, and the never-to-have-been husband and wife, might there have been a moment in which Wordsworth looked on his daughter, now herself a wife and mother, as at once the bearer of conflict *and* as a principle of restitution?

(Endnotes)

1. A FORM OF PRAYER, TO BE USED In All Churches and Chapels … upon Friday the Nineteenth of April next, being the Day appointed by Proclamation for a

General FAST and Humiliation Before Almighty God … By His Majesty's Special Command (London: Charles Eyre and Andrew Strahan, 1793), title page

2. For a detailed account of Wordsworth's publishing activities in this year see Kenneth R. Johnston, *The Hidden Wordsworth: Poet, Lover, Rebel, Spy* (New York, London: W.W. Norton, 1998), 334–40

3. A FORM OF PRAYER … (1793), 6

4. See Johnston, *The Hidden Wordsworth*, 388

5. 1805 text. Quotations are taken from William Wordsworth, *The Prelude, 1799, 1805, 1850*, ed. Jonathan Wordsworth, M.H. Abrams and Stephen Gill (New York and London: W.W. Norton, 1979)

6. Johnston, *The Hidden Wordsworth*, 388.

7. A FORM OF PRAYER AND THANKSGIVING TO ALMIGHTY GOD; TO BE USED … on Thursday the Eighteenth of January, Being the Day appointed by Proclamation for a General THANKSGIVING to Almighty God … (London: George Eyre and Andrew Strahan, 1816), 10

8. Eric C. Walker, *Marriage, Writing and Romanticism: Wordsworth and Austen After War* (Stanford: Stanford University Press, 2009), 73–8

9. Quotations from the Thanksgiving Ode are taken from William Wordsworth, *Shorter Poems, 1807–1820*, ed. Carl Ketcham (Ithaca, New York: Cornell University Press, 1989). For further commentary on Wordsworth's response to Waterloo see Philip Shaw, *Waterloo and the Romantic Imagination* (Houndmills: Palgrave Macmillan, 2002), 140–64. The discussion of contemporary reactions to 'Carnage is thy daughter' is adapted from Philip Shaw, '"On War": De Quincey's Martial Sublime', *Romanticism*, 19.1 (2013), 19–30

10. *The Complete Works of William Hazlitt*, ed. P.P. Howe, 21 vols. (London: J.M. Dent, 1930–34), IV, 347–8

11. 'Peter Bell the Third', *Shelley's Poetry and Prose*, ed. Donald H. Reiman and Sharon B. Powers (London, New York: W.W. Norton, 1977), 343–4

12. 'Don Juan', *Lord Byron: The Complete Poetical Works*, ed. Jerome J. McGann and Barry Weller, 7 vols. (Oxford: Clarendon Press, 1980–93), V, 367

13. Ibid., 732

14. *The Literary Criticism of John Ruskin*, ed. Harold Bloom (New York: De Capo Press, 1965), 371–3

15. 'Thanksgiving Ode', *The Poetical Works of William Wordsworth*, ed. Ernest de Selincourt and Helen Darbishire, 5 vols. (Oxford: Clarendon Press, 1940–49), III, 155

16. Carl Ketcham, *Shorter Poems*, 16

17. Samuel Humfrays, *The Sword is the Lord's. A Sermon Preached in the Parish-Church of Daventry, Sunday, January 19th 1794 …* (Northampton: T. Dicey, 1794), 13

18. Johnston, *The Hidden Wordsworth*, 390

After Visiting the Field of Waterloo (1820)

William Wordsworth

A WINGED Goddess, clothed in vesture wrought

Of rainbow colours; One whose port was bold,

Whose overburthened hand could scarcely hold

The glittering crowns and garlands which it brought,

Hover'd in air above the far-famed Spot.

She vanished — All was joyless, blank, and cold;

But if from wind-swept fields of corn that roll'd

In dreary billows, from the meagre cot,

And monuments that soon may disappear,

Meanings we craved which could not there be found;

If the wide prospect seemed an envious seal

Of great exploits; we felt as Men *should* feel,

With such vast hoards of hidden carnage near,

And horror breathing from the silent ground!

TURNER MEETS HIS WATERLOO: FROM SKETCHBOOK TO PICTURE

DAVID BLAYNEY BROWN

J.M.W. TURNER WAS a lifelong traveller, interested in the scenery, culture and history of the places he visited — especially when these aspects came together to lend meaning and significance to a location. Nowhere, surely, was this more the case than at Waterloo, the site of the single most decisive historical event of his generation. The Belgian battlefield was not the only object of his tour to the Netherlands and Rhineland in the summer of 1817, nor was it to be the only subject of a picture to emerge from it, but it was by far the most important — a place he came to as a history painter, a reader of history and a lover of literature, and an avowedly European artist, not merely a British landscape painter. His 1817 tour marked his return to this larger stage after years of confinement to Britain during the Napoleonic War; Waterloo was the scene of its greatest drama (see fig. 21 for a contemporary map of the battlefield of Waterloo).

As Sarah Monks, the late Fred Bachrach and other scholars have shown, Turner had a longstanding interest in Low Countries (mainly Dutch) art as a marine and genre painter which led him towards historical concerns — for example, the Anglo-Dutch wars of the 1660s.[1] His study and adoption of the luminous atmospherics of Cuyp, the stormy gloom of Ruysdael, or the recent reinvention by David Wilkie of familiar-life subjects in the manner of Ostade and Teniers gave a contemporary edge to these art-historical concerns. Partly, the 1817 trip was a chance to see where these artists had come from and what they painted. It was also a chance to measure himself against them by tackling the central subject of modern history from observations on the spot. He must have known that none had had to deal with a subject like Waterloo — unremarkable as a landscape yet tragic, epic, epoch-making in what had happened there — and only one Old Master, Rembrandt, would serve his modern purpose. But first he had to visit the field.

As always for his European tours, but perhaps more so this time as it was his first since 1802 and the first on which he travelled on his own, Turner took steps to prepare himself. He stocked up with recent guidebooks by Charles Campbell and his fellow artist Robert Hills (the last recently reissued with an extra chapter describing a 'Walk over the Field of Battle'), making notes beforehand and en route, and jotting down useful phrases. He had with him several bound sketchbooks, small enough to slip into his coat pocket. One he christened 'Itinerary Rhine Tour' [Tate, Turner Bequest

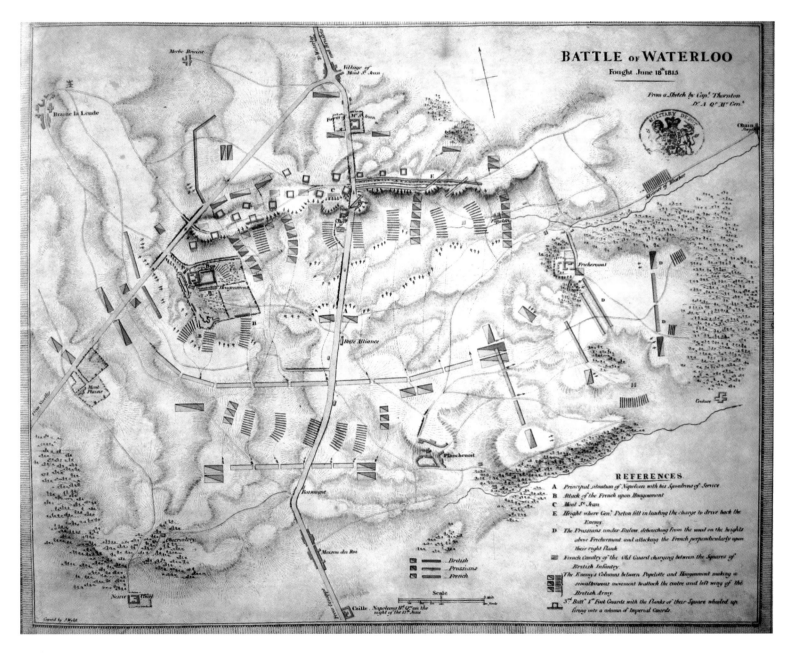

Figure 21. Map of the Battlefield of Waterloo. Belonging to David and Janet Bromley.

CLIX], another 'Waterloo and Rhine'. From the first of these it appears he left London on Sunday 10 August and sailed from Margate the next day; arrived at Ostend and travelled to Bruges on Tuesday 12; and reached Waterloo, via Ghent and Brussels, on Saturday 16. A similarly tight timetable was set for the rest of the tour, leaving little time in each place — some were revisited on the way back, but not Waterloo. So he had to work quickly, making his sketches and notes in the space of a day.

Fortunately — if also distractingly for an artist wanting to concentrate — the battlefield was becoming a tourist site, with an emerging infrastructure to match. There were regular coach services each way from Brussels, and guides — local farmers or the like — who led visitors around for a fee or a tip. Their help meant that Turner did not have to rely on his preliminary reading but could augment it with local knowledge, memories and even statistics. As Cecilia Powell has observed, while Turner sketched the battlefield in the conventional sequence of locations — arriving from the north and then walking clockwise as described in Campbell's book — he added a good deal of extra information that he must have been given on the spot.[2] Running over seventeen pages, he made a series of sketches, sometimes quick outlines, some diagrammatic and others more finished, noting details about the battle, its armies, phases and casualties (see fig. 22). Collecting this sort of memoranda when it was available came as second nature to Turner, but it is inconceivable that he was not already planning a picture. Some years earlier, he had researched his monumental painting *The Battle of Trafalgar* [Tate, London] in similar fashion, boarding the damaged *Victory* when she returned home for repairs, interviewing her remaining crew and filling a sketchbook with sketches, notes and diagrams of the order of battle — some of which might even have been contributed by men he met on board.[3] As one turns the leaves of these books two centuries seem to vanish in a moment and history comes alive.

From Brussels, Turner's coach deposited him at the village of Waterloo. There, he sketched the domed Royal Chapel from the inn that the British commander, the Duke of Wellington, had used as his rear headquarters. It was an appropriate starting-point. Then he set off southwards across the burnt and blasted wasteland, traversed by causeways that the troops had used during the battle and still scarred by the ruins of the farms of La Haye Sainte, La Belle Alliance and Hougoumont, which formed a rough triangle at its centre and was where the fiercest fighting took place. This was Belgium, and the battlefield was at best a gently undulating plain, but good views could be had from Mont St-Jean, where the British and their German allies took up their stations. Turner made close studies of the three farms and noted their positions in relation to each other and the progress of the battle. La Haye Sainte and the large manor farm of Hougoumont, set between the allied and French lines, had covered the allied advance and were attacked all day by the French. Hougoumont, bombarded and ablaze, had held out to the last. La Belle Alliance, on the French front line, was the location of the meeting of the allied leaders on the evening after the French were defeated. By a view of La Haye from the south, Turner noted '4000 killed here; Line of E[nglish]; Orchard; Picton killed here; 1500 killed here', and so on; another sketch nearby records the famous 'Picton tree' where Sir Thomas Picton died — the most senior British officer lost on the field. To one of his last views of Hougoumont Turner added a diagram of the fighting there, noting 'Entrance Gate of Hugumont forced

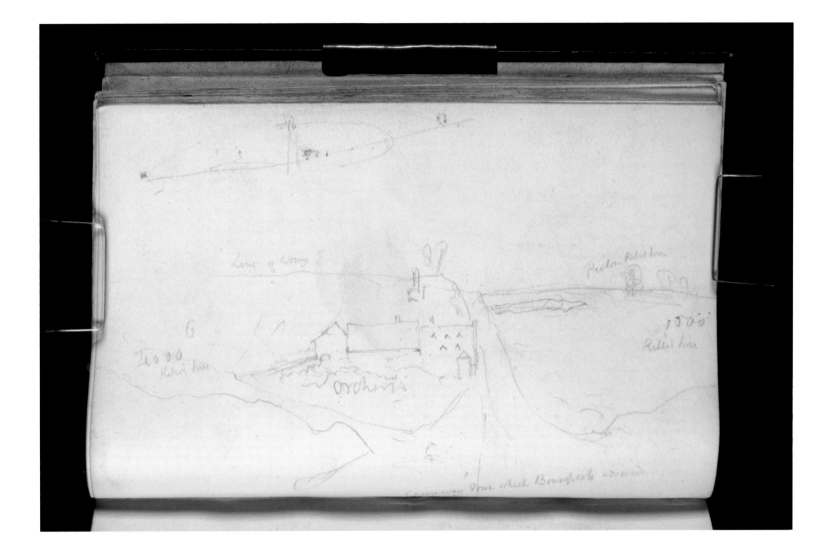

Figure 22. Joseph Mallord William Turner (1775–1851), from *Waterloo and Rhine Sketchbook*, 1817. © Tate, London 2015.

4 times; Picton [again]; Causeway to Belle … Hollow where the great Carnage took place of the Cuirassiers by the Guards' — the Scots and Coldstreams whose refusal to yield despite terrible losses had finally turned the battle. Presumably later on, while collecting more detail for his picture, Turner sketched uniforms in another 'Guards' sketchbook [Tate, Turner Bequest CLXIV].

Local memories of these terrible events must still have been fresh and traumatic even if the dead were buried (or burnt) and the corn was growing back. That presumably the field was not quite empty and Turner came across other visitors cannot have diminished its desolation. His impressions had time to settle as he still had most of his tour ahead of him; onward via the Rhine, from Cologne to Mainz and back, thence to Antwerp homeward across Holland. In Amsterdam he had noted, as a must-see, Rembrandt's 'Corps de Guarde'. This, of course, was *The Night Watch* [Rijksmuseum, Amsterdam], with its striking effects of chiaroscuro. Already a long-standing admirer of the Dutch master, Turner had praised these very qualities to the Royal Academy in his lectures as its Professor of Perspective, describing how Rembrandt 'depended upon … his bursts of light and darkness to be felt' and could transform even the 'most objectionable' subjects by 'matchless colour'.[4] Although its polar opposite, a supreme celebration of civic culture in a peaceful, orderly, democratic society, *The Night Watch* can only have confirmed these opinions and pointed towards the tonal and colouristic repertoire needed for the picture Turner was planning. This was not a picture of the battle, or the moment of victory, but a compassionate visualisation of its aftermath, when dead and dying litter the field and women — wives, lovers, mothers — search for their menfolk by torchlight. Whether intended to deter looters or aid search parties, a

flare lighting up the sky strikes an almost apocalyptic note, white and hard against the duller glow cast by the still-burning ruins of Hougoumont (see fig. 23). Caught in the various lights, sparks of intense colour — red, white and gold uniforms and standards, a yellow drum, silver breastplates — burst out of the dark. From the jumble of bodies, faces emerge frozen in pain.

The previous year, 1816, the British Institution had announced a competition for a picture celebrating the allied victory at Waterloo, with a suitably patriotic, Anglocentric work in mind. Turner's picture was not remotely in this mould; indeed, exhibited at the Royal Academy two years later, it amounts to a rebuff to organised jingoism. Instead, his impressions of Waterloo were mediated through Byron's famous lines in Canto III of *Childe Harold's Pilgrimage* describing the run-up to the battle, the Duchess of Richmond's ball in Brussels the previous evening, the 'stern array' of fighting and then — as he painted — 'Rider and horse — friend, foe — in one red burial blent!' This mingling of the dead and the opposing armies is, if anything, even clearer in Turner's slightly later watercolour of the subject [Fitzwilliam Museum, Cambridge], where a gun-carriage is stamped 'GR III' (George III) and a saddlecloth bears the initial 'N' (Napoleon). The watercolour lacks the searching women and seems to be set in daylight; this time, however, the drama of battle is figured by other very Turnerian motifs of strife, a storm and lightning flashes, in this context again evoking Byron: 'The thunder-clouds rose o'er it, which when rent / The earth is cover'd thick with other clay'. Later, returning to the essentials of his painting, Turner reinterpreted his Byronic image as a design (engraved by Edward Finden) for a title vignette for volume XIV of the collected *Life and Works of Byron*, where it illustrated

Figure 23. Joseph Mallord William Turner (1775–1851), *The Field of Waterloo*, 1818. © Tate, London 2015.

'bloody and most bootless Waterloo' from *The Age of Bronze*. He also provided a pre-battle depiction of *Hougoumont* to illustrate Walter Scott's *Miscellaneous Prose*.

Despite this later literary legacy for Turner's treatment of Waterloo, the picture was panned when first exhibited, presumably because it failed to celebrate its subject or represent victory at all. For the *Annals of the Fine Arts* it was no more than a 'drunken hubbub on an illumination night'.[5] It was left to Hazlitt, most perspicacious and visually acute of critics, to praise Turner's 'magical illustration of how at nightfall there was only left the fiery explosions and carnage after the battle, when the wives and brothers and sons of the slain come, with anxious eyes and agonized hearts, to look at Ambition's charnel-house'.[6] Clearly, Hazlitt had really looked hard at the picture. Turner's politics are mysterious and we cannot know if he shared the radical Hazlitt's despair — signalled by wearing a black armband after Waterloo — at the loss of what had seemed to him a European force for progress embodied by Napoleon as much as at the loss of life. But we can certainly allow Turner compassion and feeling for what was as much a human tragedy as a victory. This rises above the taking of sides, let alone the painterly achievement of a striking visual effect. Turner's *Waterloo* — like the shipwrecked slaves or drowning female convicts who appear in his later pictures — is surely the product of that wider Romantic sympathy for the victims of history that had, extraordinarily, produced a similar image from the very heart of the Napoleonic elite: Baron Gros' *Battlefield of Eylau* [Louvre, Paris]. It seems just as extraordinary that Turner cannot have seen this picture, exhibited in 1808, as he had not since been to Paris, for despite the prominence given to the Emperor, visiting the field the day after the battle, there is the same foreground strewn with foreshortened corpses and intense realism in the depiction of death. Perhaps Turner knew of Wellington's remark, as he surveyed Waterloo, that nothing except a battle lost can be half so melancholy as a battle won.

(Endnotes)

1. Sarah Monks, 'Turner Goes Dutch', in David Solkin ed., *Turner and the Masters*, exhibition catalogue, Tate Britain (London: Tate Publishing, 2009), 73–85; Fred G.H. Bachrach, *Turner's Holland*, exhibition catalogue, Tate Gallery (London: Tate Publishing, 1994)

2. Cecilia Powell, *Turner's Rivers of Europe: The Rhine, Meuse and Mosel*, exhibition catalogue, Tate Gallery (London: Tate Publishing, 1991), 23–4

3. The 'Nelson' sketchbook (Tate, Turner Bequest LXXXIX)

4. Turner in Jerrold Ziff, 'Backgrounds: Introduction of Architecture and Landscape', *Journal of the Warburg and Courtauld Institutes*, 26 (1963), 145; also Monks (2009), 79

5. Cited by Martin Butlin and Evelyn Joll, *The Paintings of J.M.W. Turner* (New Haven, London: Yale University Press, rev. 1984), 93

6. *The Examiner*, 24 May 1818

My whole soul was with those who were resolved

to fight it out with Bonaparte

William Wordsworth to Henry Crabb Robinson, 2 August 1816

GRAPHIC SATIRE IN THE AGE OF NAPOLEON & WELLINGTON

DONALD COVERDALE

THE REIGNS OF George III and George IV have rightly been called the Golden Age of Caricature. Artists such as James Gillray, Thomas Rowlandson and George Cruikshank were early practitioners of an art form that has endured to the present day. Their brightly coloured prints that were sold in a handful of print shops in the West End of London were expensive items that could only be bought by an affluent upper class, but they appealed to a wide audience who were able to gather in the street and share the humour which they could see displayed in the shop windows of Hannah Humphrey, Samuel Fores, William Holland and others. James Gillray (1756–1815) was the greatest caricaturist of his age and the creator of many images which have endured in the minds of connoisseurs (with a sense of humour) for over two hundred years.

These prints were sold individually or in batches and print sellers were willing to hire out folios of prints by the evening. They could be produced fairly quickly following important events of the day, the artist sometimes drawing his ideas directly on to a copper plate which was then used to create prints by passing individual sheets of paper through the printing press (a laborious process) prior to hand colouring which, in the case of Gillray's prints, was done by a team of women who exercised particular care in the process. Other print sellers used children for the colouring process but the result was frequently crude and did little credit to the artist.

Gillray's prints were sold for about half-a-crown coloured or one shilling plain. To place these sums in perspective, for much of this period unskilled labourers were fortunate to be earning as much as ten shillings a week. Sometimes these standard prices were reduced for plates which had been subsidised as propaganda. Unusually large compositions were generally offered at five shillings.

From the outbreak of the French Revolution until the end of his career in 1810 much of Gillray's political output was concerned with the momentous events in France and the subsequent long and enduring wars with the French. His prints, being aimed at a popular market, initially appeared sympathetic to the aims of the Revolution. However, as Terror raged in France and the guillotine began to rise and fall, so public opinion began to turn. An early display of revulsion at the execution of Louis XVI is *The Zenith of French Glory; — The Pinnacle of Liberty* of 1793 (fig. 24). France declared war on Britain and Holland; Gillray's print appeared twelve days

Figure 24. James Gillray (1756–1815), *The Zenith of French Glory; — The Pinnacle of Liberty*, 1793.

© Trustees of the British Museum.

later. It is a vivid image, being one of Gillray's most memorable prints: there is much detail in the foreground figures which are highly worked up; the viewer is left with a lasting impression of the horrors of the Revolution and the outrages committed by the sans-culottes. In this one print we see the tricolour ('Vive L'Egalité'), the guillotine, the bonnet rouge, the treatment meted out to monks, a bishop and a judge and a crucifix adorned with a piece of paper reading 'Bon Soir Monsieur' above a skull and crossbones. The sans-culotte, his bare behind balanced on the lantern and his foot on the bishop's neck, is one of Gillray's most telling inventions.

Hatred and contempt of the French remained a theme of the caricatures published throughout the war years. Particular derision was heaped upon Napoleon who was depicted as a diminutive maniac prone to histrionics in *Maniac Raving's — or — Little Boney in a strong Fit* of 1803 (fig. 25) and as a victim of the Devil who roasts him in Hell in *The Corsican-Pest; — or — Belzebub going to Supper*, also of 1803 (fig. 26). Both of these prints merit a careful study of the detail. The eight verses below the latter are full of coarse invective, the third and sixth reading as follows:

> Belzebub will rejoice, at a Supper so nice,
> And make all his Devils feast Hearty,
> But the little-tit-bit, on a fork, he would spit
> The Consular Chief Buonaparte!

> Full Rotten the Heart of the said Buonaparte,
> Corrupted his marrow and Bones,

Figure 25. James Gillray (1756–1815), *Maniac Raving's — or — Little Boney in a strong Fit*, 1803. © Trustees of the British Museum.

Figure 26. James Gillray (1756–1815), *The Corsican-Pest; — or — Belzebub going to Supper*, 1803. © Trustees of the British Museum.

French Evil o'erflows, from his Head to his Toes,

And disorder'd his Brains in his Sconce!

The final verse no doubt added a welcome touch of loyalty to the dear King George III:

By the Favor of Heaven, to Our Monarch is given

The power to avert such dire evil,

His Subjects are ready, all Loyal & Steady

To hurl this damn'd Pest to the Devil.

This was just what the public wanted. Napoleon's likely fate in the event of an invasion of England is graphically illustrated in *Buonaparte, 48 hours after Landing* of 1803 (fig. 27): John Bull holds aloft the head of Napoleon impaled on a pitchfork, the consequence of threatening 'Old England's Roast-Beef & Plumpudding'.

The character of John Bull, representing the stout Englishman, features in numerous caricatures. He is sometimes compared to the French who had to endure an apparent diet of raw onions and raw snails while John enjoyed his roast beef, tankards of beer and the comforts of the home hearth. He frequently appears blotched with drink, gorging on his beef and complaining bitterly about the burdens of taxes and interference by the state. Plus ça change.

John Bulls Progress of 1793 (fig. 12) shows John in a far more cynical scenario, progressing from comfortable family life to enthusiastic enlistment as he marches off with a troop of soldiers; then his wife and children are reduced to a state of penury as they resort to a pawnbroker (The Treasury), and have to give up the spinning wheel and all household goods. Finally John returns home, a gaunt, one legged and one-eyed soldier in tattered uniform, confronting his starving family. Usually John Bull is portrayed as a figure of peace who is rarely aggressive and exists primarily as an object for harassment and exploitation, his tormentors being his leaders at home and not his enemies abroad. On this occasion Gillray's sympathy for enlisted men will have been intensified by the fact that his father lost an arm at Fontenoy in 1745 and by the recollection of his boyhood spent in the shadow of the Royal Military Hospital at Chelsea, where his father had been a patient and pensioner from 1746 to 1754.

The humiliation of Napoleon was complete with the publication in 1805 of *The Grand Coronation Procession of Napoleone the 1st Emperor of France, from the Church of Notre-Dame Decr 2d 1804* (fig. 6). This is an elaborate and ludicrous parody of the ridiculous pomp and ceremony surrounding Napoleon's coronation. He appears as a small figure, accompanied by a gross Josephine, and is half suffocated by the carnival excess of his robes. Talleyrand is cruelly depicted with his deformed foot prominent. Legend has it that Napoleon could not see this print 'without entering into the most violent anger'.

In 1808 Gillray produced *Spanish-Patriots attacking the French Banditti* (fig. 8), depicting events at the recent Battle of Sierra Morena. The Spanish had routed the French who eventually surrendered with 18,000 Frenchmen laying down their arms. There had been no English involvement in Spain at that time but Gillray could not resist commenting on the dispatch of Napoleon's army: his terrified soldiers are

Figure 27. James Gillray (1756–1815), *Buonaparte, 48 hours after Landing*, 1803.

Figure 28. James Gillray (1756–1815), *The Plumb-pudding in danger; — or — State Epicures taking un Petit Souper*, 1805. © Trustees of the British Museum.

depicted as suffering at the hands of both Spanish forces and a single British soldier.

While most of Gillray's caricatures contain significant detail in the narrative, the speech bubbles and skilful composition in some are striking because of the simplicity of their imagery and the message that they were intended to convey. *The Plumb-pudding in danger; — or — State Epicures taking un Petit Souper* of 1805 (fig. 28) is arguably the most famous caricature of all time. It is a universal image of the realities of power: the British Prime Minister William Pitt, with a knife and a trident-shaped fork, carves from the steaming plum-pudding a great slice of 'Ocean' while a ferocious Napoleon helps himself to Europe — a brilliant illustration of the respective areas of power of the two countries.

Gillray ceased work in 1810 when he lapsed into insanity, possibly associated with his intemperate habits. He died on the 1st June 1815, seventeen days before the battle of Waterloo. His incapacity prevented him from passing any comment upon Wellington, but the work of other caricaturists continued with the Iron Duke becoming a particular target. The perception that he was less successful as a politician than as a soldier pervaded the prints and his image moved gradually from huge affection and respect to unpleasant implications that he had ambitions to wear the royal crown or to become England's dictator. The world of politics inevitably exposed him to the ridicule which all politicians suffer at the hands of satirists, and the comparatively few caricatures concerning his military career were far outnumbered by political ribaldry in his later life. 'Waterloo Man' became a term of opprobrium, and it was generally realised that a military training did not necessarily act as a satisfactory apprenticeship for a career as a statesmen.

In the 1830s, print shops and caricatures were becoming less popular: illustrated newspapers and satirical magazines were taking their place and, being produced in large quantities, they could be accessed by a wider public. Victorian values marked their further decline as an art form. However we can, today, still enjoy the irreverent and scurrilous output of these fathers of the modern cartoon. Eighteenth-and nineteenth-century caricatures were undoubtedly more than mere ephemera.